LIVING ON AN ISLAND

LIVING ON AN ISLAND

Vicki Coleman and Ruth Wheeler

THE THULE PRESS

The publishers gratefully acknowledge
the financial assistance of the Scottish Arts
Council in the production of this book.

First published 1980
© Ruth Wheeler and Vicki Coleman 1980
ISBN 0 906191 55 6

Set in 11/13 point Journal Roman
Designed by Neil Baird
Printed and bound by Unwin Brothers Ltd.
Published by The Thule Press, Findhorn, Moray

If Once You Have Slept On An Island
By Rachel Field

If once you have slept on an island
  You'll never be quite the same;
You may look as you looked the day before
  And go by the same old name.

You may bustle about in street or shop;
  You may sit at home and sew,
But you'll see blue water and wheeling gulls
  Wherever your feet may go.

You may chat with the neighbours of this and that
  And close to your fire keep,
But you'll hear ship whistle and lighthouse bell
  And tides beat through your sleep.

Oh, you won't know why, and you can't say how
  Such a change upon you came,
But—once you have slept on an island
  You'll never be quite the same!

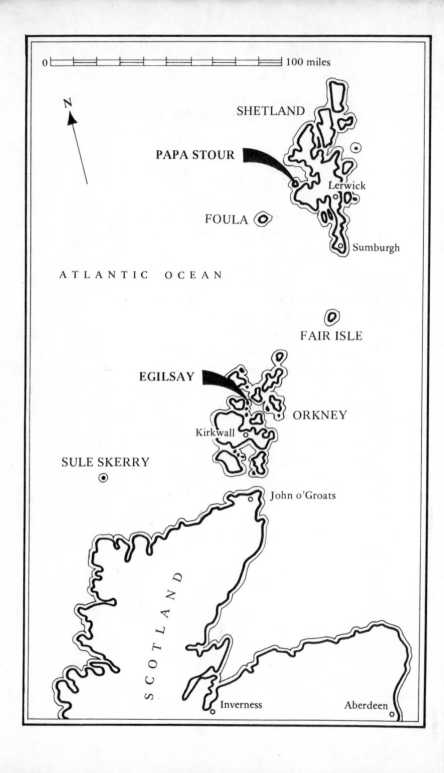

Contents

PART ONE
EGILSAY

Ruth Wheeler

Chapter 1
Why an island?

What a question! I still don't know the answer. On a rare day of good weather when Egilsay rests like a brilliant emerald jewel in an azure sea the answer seems just within my grasp. Today as I write, my hands numb, a foot of snow outside and sleet hurtling horizontally past the window, I am sure of nothing.

However, part of the answer must lie back in Brighton where we lived five years ago. We had a nice house, nice car, nice jobs, nice baby, so what was wrong with us? I could trot out the cliches like 'disenchantment with urban life', 'a desire to be self-sufficient', or 'fed up with the rat race', but in truth we didn't know what was wrong with us. We'd never heard of 'self-sufficiency' and I doubt that we'd ever analysed our feelings about the urban chaos which surrounded us. That initial decision to alter the course of one's life is such a tenuous moment, such a uniquely personal thing that it belies description and analysis. How can I tell you? Perhaps it is the moment when one knows for certain that one cannot get on that same bus or train each morning, or the moment when one realises with panic that over half of one's allotted fourscore years have passed without incident.

For us, I think it may have been just about 'people' — too many, too often in places like our home where we didn't particularly wish to see them. I cannot remember the precise moment when I said "Enough!", but I do recall that there was distinct difference in the flavour of life once that decision had been made. All our leisure time was devoted to scanning such publications as the *Farmers Weekly* and *Exchange & Mart*. We took time off work, piled into the car — dog, baby, supplies and all — and started the long search. We didn't find anywhere suitable but we got to know an awful lot of people and some very interesting parts of Devon, Cornwall, Wales, the South Eastern Counties, Durham, Yorkshire and Scotland. We also began to read avidly. We were fired with the kind of idealistic zeal that now comes in such small and infrequent doses that I have to be at peak awareness in order to exploit it! We absorbed every word which John Seymour and others like him penned, never pausing to ask the obvious question: how can anyone grow everything, shoot everything, bottle it, bake bread, and still find time to write?

After absorbing all the literature on the simple life, we decided that it had to be total self-sufficiency or nothing. And so as we cast off television, washing machine and other mod cons, our once nice house became a dumping ground for old oil lamps, iron cooking utensils, butter churns and other assorted paraphernalia. The neighbours gave us a wide berth. One friend who managed to remain faithful during these difficult times used to accompany me on sorties to local rubbish tips where we retrieved old tin baths and similar treasures. We transported them back to the house on push chairs with bored, fractious toddlers trailing behind. In a house reeking of charred bread, failed jam and pickling vinegar we discussed man's inhumanity towards the environment, his fellow creatures, land wastage and other such lofty subjects. After a year or so it was as if we had dressed for a party but were minus the invitation, and when all hope seemed to be lost we suddenly discovered that there were islands to the north of Scotland as well as to the west. We scanned an old school atlas for some likely looking names and came up with Kirkwall and Lerwick which seemed to be in bold type. With his usual flair my husband Jan had a brilliant idea: why not write to estate agents in Orkney and Shetland? A friend who had grown up in Scotland informed us that it was customary for lawyers to handle property sales in this part of the world. Taking this sound advice we penned two letters asking for information on any small farms or crofts in the area. But we didn't know the names or addresses of any solicitors! "Not to worry," said Jan, as he confidently stuck down the two envelopes. I saw him scribbling something on the envelopes. . .

To: Any Solicitor   To: Any Solicitor
     Kirkwall   Lerwick
     Orkney   Shetland

     and. . .

I must award full marks to the Post Office in Kirkwall, for they made sure that the letter reached the offices of a local solicitor. He contacted us promptly, almost by return of post. We received details of a thirty acre holding on the mainland of Orkney for £400. We could hardly believe our luck, and phoned immediately to say that the deal was done. It wasn't. The letter contained a £3,600 typing error. The price was £4,000; still good value, but we hesitated and all was lost. After two or three weeks of waiting another letter arrived with details of 'Whistlebare', a thirteen acre croft on the island of Egilsay, eleven miles north of Orkney mainland. Within two days Jan was on his way to see it and I was waiting anxiously for his phone call. When he rang he was brief and to the point. "It's in a beautiful position, overlooking a sound with a good sea frontage. The house is abysmal and needs a hell of a lot of work if not completely rebuilding." After a lot of "What do you think then?" and "No, you decide," we made the decision to go ahead. Of course we didn't ask questions like: "What is the population now and what was it ten or twenty years ago?" "Why are people leaving?" "How many kids are there in the school?" "What's the transport situation?" and "What about the climate and what can one grow there?"

Thus without being fully aware at the time we chose a part of Britain where a total or even semi-self-reliance is almost impossible, and where winter lasts for nine months of the year. We chose a spot on the island where hurricane force westerly winds nearly blast us off the face of the earth in the winter, and a place with virtually no services and amenities.

But we came and are still here.

We stayed because on those few elusive days of peace and calm, when the sound is like a millpond and the gulls dip and dive into a topaz sea in the wake of a creeling boat, when the cattle and goats lazily munch the rich blue-green grass over which Egilsay seems to have exclusive franchise, then we know we have found our paradise. The next day a gale will be battering down the vegetables, the water pump will have broken down and generator stopped working; but just when we are about to take the first offer on the place, the island will yet again offer us a tantalising glimpse of heaven—a spectacular sunset or breathtaking dawn which tugs at our sleeves and says tauntingly, "You won't leave."

Back in Brighton in 1974 I knew nothing of these confused and conflicting emotions. My frustrations lay in more mundane areas like the bus being late or the supermarket being out of our usual brand of baked beans. Little did I know that I was about to be exposed to such a range of emotions and frustrations that after a while I would hardly recognise myself.

Once the Brighton house was sold we had several months to fill in before taking over Whistlebare. We nursed idealistic dreams of carrying water from the well and lighting oil lamps. We fed our dreams on a diet of do-it-yourself manuals and second-hand stories of friends of friends who had done it. We listened to relatives who had come fairly near to supporting themselves in Africa, discovering too late the extent to which Africa and Orkney differ. Fate dealt with us kindly in one respect, for we were able to take over the post office which the former occupant of the croft had run. The salary was low but would keep us from total starvation. Also, because we had not gone to the limit of our capital from the Brighton house, we had something to spare for emergencies.

On Wednesday, July 29th, we set off on the journey north. Our twenty-two hundredweight van bulged at the seams with all manner of tools and utensils designed to make the simple life simpler. We had sold a houseful of beautiful antiques — some for a song at the very last minute. We had well and truly cast off the trappings of civilisation. It was a catharsis and we felt very noble and cleansed, a little less acquisitive and parasitic. Unfortunately, the owners of guest houses and other establishments did not quite appreciate the nobility of our motives. When a dusty yellow van rolled up with tin baths strapped to the roof rack, and a smelly dog followed by an even smellier baby and two jaded adults, the 'No Vacancy' signs went up pretty swiftly. Farther north people were less ruled by convention and the welcome was warmer. In some places we were the star attraction as we regaled the other guests with tales of our great adventure. Families from such far-flung places as Scunthorpe and Stoke-on-Trent told us of how they had been just about to do it but were held back at the eleventh hour by her mother, or Dad's job, or the eldest's A levels. It seemed that inside everyone there was an Edmund Hillary or John Ridgeway struggling to get out.

At half past five on August 1st we boarded the *Islander* docked at Kirkwall Pier. Until that moment I had not been in touch with reality. It was all a dream. I had been lost in a frenzy of preparation and travelling. Suddenly it hit me. I was leaving behind everything and everyone I knew. To us this was totally uncharted territory.

A mass of strange faces stared up as we disembarked at Egilsay pier. Because we were the first English pioneers they were naturally curious, if not pretty sceptical. As I approached Whistlebare along a rough track from the pier I felt as if I were in a surrealist picture. I didn't belong there. The place was wild, the grass long and coarse and rough stone buildings with their roofs of stone and thatch were relics from another age.

As Jan opened the door reality slapped me in the face. Two huge box beds took up much of the available space. There was one room in which we were to carry out all the normal functions of everyday life. I looked up to see bare rafters blackened by a hundred years or more of smoke from the fire and oil from the lamps. They were the only support between me and the massive stone roofing slabs. Then I looked down at the floor, huge uneven chunks of rock laid directly down on the earth which oozed up between them. In a state of total shock I ventured timidly inside. There in the ancient fireplace stood a blackened monster with great claw-like feet, a fire still smouldering in the grate. I walked over to the box bed and lifted up an old grey army blanket. It revealed a chaff mattress on which we were to sleep that night. The most basic of all human instincts nearly overwhelmed me, to run like hell back to the pier and board any boat which would put some distance between me and this dreadful place. But there was to be no turning back.

After the first half hour I found myself moving about mechanically, sorting out pots and pans and fetching water from the well in order to make a much needed cup of tea. On reflection, I may have been suffering from something euphemistically called culture shock. It's a state of mind which overtakes all of us who try to persuade ourselves that there is something more noble, more worthwhile about living in a damp, smoke-filled hovel rather than a comfortable home, or eating food totally alien to our palates, its one and only virtue being that it is home produced. But on that brilliant August morning I was still moved by the spirit, sure that the sacrifices were more than worthwhile.

To complicate the issue even more an official had appeared from Kirkwall to supervise the taking over of the Post Office. The actual Post Office building, a tiny hut, looked as if it had been fashioned by the same architect who had designed the house. The wood was rotting and the door had to be closed very carefully in order to prevent the total collapse of the edifice. Re-roofing had obviously been a dirty word around the place and the one and only way to hold off the ravages of time and weather was to throw a little more vegetation on the dwelling house and plaster another layer of tar on the Post Office roof. Unfortunately the roofing expert had not bothered to fill the cracks and holes before embarking on the tar job, and the black treacly substance cascading down the inside walls looked like an over-iced birthday cake. Yet it did hold everything together both inside and out, even the official notices on the walls, some of which dated from the Great War.

In the confusion of settling in I hadn't even found time to examine the outbuildings, and it was toward the end of the first week when I found time to walk around and take in our folly. The outbuildings consisted of a byre to house three or four cattle, a small stable, and a barn in which we found a huge, immovable hand mill. The barn had been used for the threshing and storage of grain in the old days. The stable was next to useless and we used it as the lavatory, but the byre and barn were in reasonable order, in many ways better than the dwelling house.

The land was wild and untamed, ungrazed for close on twenty years. We ached to get livestock on it, and one of our first moves was to advertise for goats. The replies poured in, some for the taking and few over the princely sum of £5. Knowing nothing about goats didn't help, but I was lucky in my choices. I bought an Alpine for £2 who turned out to be a winner — a gallon-a-day goat—and two Saanens at £5 each who were not quite so good as Heidi, the Alpine, but still excellent value.

Heidi was a one-woman goat, balky and ill-tempered with everyone else but behaving like a dream for me. At night when she was settled in the byre I would go down, bucket and tilley lamp in hand. She stood absolutely still to be milked, and so great was the rapport between us that it precluded the use of verbal signs. I never had occasion to speak harshly to her and she seemed to know instinctively what I expected. For the first and perhaps the only time in my life I knew the joy which arises from a perfect working relationship with an animal. When she died a couple of years later, it seemed that a precious yet tenuous link with this place had been abruptly and cruelly broken.

In the five years we have been here goats, cattle, hens, sheep and geese have come and gone, some via the pier, others deposited in the deep freeze. Perhaps we have become more blasé about our dealings with animals, hardened and less starry-eyed about the whole business, but I cannot recreate the relationship which existed between myself and the first of the four-legged occupants of Whistlebare.

Chapter 2
Where shall we begin?

When we arrived, this question plagued us day and night. The grass was waist high and the building was primitive. Our first attack was on the garden, which we dug over and surrounded with a dry stone wall four feet high. It should have been six feet but our back muscles and enthusiasm began to flag, especially in the wind and rain. The rain had a nasty habit of finding its way into every nook and cranny of the house. After several months of sleepless nights listening to water plop into buckets we decided that the squalor was too much to tolerate. We took the cowardly way out and bought a mobile home. It contained everything: carpets, plumbing and electrical wiring, not to mention a gleaming white lavatory! We shut the door of the old dwelling house and it remained closed until 1977, when we felt mentally and physically capable of tackling the building work.

Maybe it was a bad idea to leave the building for so long. Perhaps we should have attacked it during that first flush of noble idealism. But the pioneering spirit goes hand in hand with a shocked numbness and a total disorientation. All newcomers feel this way, or so they tell me. They have the energy and the enthusiasm, but they lack the basic knowledge, experience and settled objectivity to channel their energies. So in many ways I'm happy that we waited before starting on the house. We decided that first we needed food, and therefore the preparation and planting of a growing area was essential. As well as the garden next to the house we ploughed up a large field, plastering it with seaweed brought up from the beach in a wheelbarrow.

In 1974 we grew little, apart from some hurriedly planted cabbages which thrived against all odds. But 1975 was a good year. We had managed in the spring to erect and reinforce a nine by twelve foot greenhouse, and we had excellent crops of tomatoes and cucumbers. Our vegetables thrived, and the newly acquired freezer bulged at the seams by the end of the growing season. The house looked like a greengrocers and smelled like a pickling factory.

When we weren't weeding, harvesting, scything oats or milking goats, we were putting up fences. In the beginning we found great joy in keeping animals — any animals. We carried far too many livestock and soon learned that this could be a disaster. Early in 1975 we tried our hand at calf rearing with disastrous results. To begin with we bought in Ayrshire crosses, a breed wholly despised by the beef men of Orkney. It was only the high calf subsidy that year which saved us from a severe financial loss. We soon learned not to dabble in agri-business, and since that time we have kept everything on a fairly small scale. We made a conscious decision not to become involved in producing beef for others. Though we might be compelled for economic reasons to sell the odd calf, we decided that meat for our own consumption should be reared and slaughtered here.

Unfortunately, and again for economic reasons, all farmers on the island are involved in medium and large scale beef production. Families come here with the idea of leaving behind the hustle and bustle of business life and, hey presto, before their feet touch the ground they are well and truly in the agricultural rat race. They worry about how many cattle can be kept over the winter, how many breeding cows they will have in 1990 and how the hell they're going to pay off the overdraft. Because we only have thirteen acres we cannot and do not concern ourselves with such matters. It may be that the place is understocked with its handful of domestic animals and assorted wildlife, but why should I have sleepless nights worrying about someone else's Sunday roast? Now if any animal consumes more time, energy and food than it is worth it must go. We only have the essentials — poultry, one goat and a milking cow, and for part of the year we keep a few sheep who usually end up in the deep freeze.

By 1977 the land was fairly well under control. We had areas fenced off for growing vegetables and crops and could at last stop to assess our situation. The moment of truth arrived. Had we enough courage to start on the house? After many arguments and agonies we tore up the flags and pulled down rotting beams of the sagging roof.

At this juncture I must say a few words about our method of working, our *modus vivendi*. Many people have to be fired with enthusiasm before they can embark upon a task, but who can summon up enthusiasm about a rotten, damp, rat-infested hovel? We certainly couldn't, and most of the work on the island seems to be of this nature, mentally and physically exhausting. So we start out in a different way. We whip ourselves into a frenzy of hatred for the task, and then the adrenalin begins to flow. We hate the rocks we are heaving, the cement we're mixing and wood we're sawing. We curse and swear and we work like beings possessed. At the end of a ten or twelve hour day the feeling of satisfied exhaustion is indescribable. We sleep like logs. The next day isn't nearly so bad, and the days after, when the results of our labours become apparent and our muscles have become attuned to the gruelling work, are almost easy.

After a couple of years of such labours we have a kind of a house. It's long, rambling and primitive with all sorts of bits and pieces attached, but I'm satisfied. I have a love/hate relationship with it. Some days I look upon our handiwork with pride: the beautiful stonework, the pine beams. Its very unevenness is a joy to behold. But in a gale when the west wind drives the rain under the still untiled roof, I wonder what sort of effort we would have to put into a shelter in order to keep the weather out.

I called this chapter 'Where shall we begin?' not just because I wanted to tell you how we started the venture, but because we repeat these words every day. Each new day is a new beginning on Egilsay; there is no middle or end. We change, our hopes and aspirations change, and the island changes constantly. To write about such a place is like trying to ensnare a wild and beautiful creature who has no intention of yielding to captivity.

Chapter 3

The island disease

Perhaps disease is too strong a word for it; perhaps I should call it an affliction. But whatever its name, its existence cannot be denied. It overtakes the unsuspecting newcomer in stages and varies in intensity. One arrives here armed with much zeal and idealism and the first thing which manifests itself is stark reality. Housing on Egilsay is either primitive or nonexistent, so the first task is usually to provide oneself with basic shelter. In most parts of Britain, this wouldn't be too much of a problem. One is usually within travelling distance of the do-it-yourself shop or the builder or the wood merchant. It's not so easy on Egilsay. There aren't any shops. You can either go to the mainland for materials, weather and boatman permitting, or you must wait for the steamer to bring the stuff, and the steamer only comes once a week. The problem of procuring building materials is one of the first frustrations of what is likely to be a very frustrating life unless one can come to terms with it. When we arrived we had no piped water or generator, so we spent many wasted hours heaving up buckets of water and fiddling around with oil lamps. Even those who come with a generator must know how the thing works, otherwise they are likely to be plunged into darkness at any time.

The newcomer doesn't take too kindly to these revelations, and it is a common sight to see such a person stomping up and down the pier, cursing and tearing his hair. But one soon learns that one is at the mercy of just about everything and everyone — a far cry from the self-reliant dream which brings one to the island in the first place.

So the food hasn't arrived, the building materials are not on the steamer, the generator has broken down and you can't plough because it's rained for three solid weeks. It is now that you wonder if this might be a conspiracy designed to break your spirit. The pioneering fervour begins to ebb, and the first symptoms of island disease begin to show. The victim wanders around, unable to concentrate on anything but commiseration with fellow sufferers. But talking about it doesn't help; the only thing that can stave off the secondary stages of the disease is prompt action. Victims must fix their attention on something else and follow it through to the bitter end — difficult for all but those with a cast-iron will.

To begin with, the island looks like a haven of peace and tranquillity. The unsuspecting visitor imagines that days here last forever and that time is endless. We were recently visited by some folk who contemplated buying a farm on the island. "One thing which strikes us immediately," they told us, "is that on every farm we see there are a hundred and one half-finished jobs. We could never live like that!" We could only manage a wry smile. How could we tell them about the island disease? How could we tell them that on the day when you might want to finish the byre, a gale wind would blow up and whip the cement over to the other side of the island? How would they understand that we had been waiting for three months to get the tiles on the roof, that every time we went to the pier the boat was late or didn't turn up at all? Who but one's fellow sufferers could understand?

After a few years the build-up of such frustrations brings about a crisis in the affliction. A decision must be made: major surgery or acceptance. Yes, one can pack up and leave the place, and many have, but the solution which most people adopt is a happy-go-lucky acceptance of the blight. Chaos takes over and things are allowed just to tick over.

The disease can take other forms. If you live in any town or city or even a large village, it's likely that you have different groups of friends and acquaintances. You have a few people with whom you play tennis or squash and maybe a less energetic group with whom you discuss politics, then when you feel like having a party you can then go and see another, more gregarious crowd. If for some reason you can't stand someone in the tennis club, you can choose not to see them for a while. You can even go to a party of the Young Socialists and tell them how sporty people are so awful.

Island life isn't like that. People come here imagining that life on an isolated island can solve all of their problems, especially those of relating to other human beings. Here one is thrust into a small world measuring three miles by one mile with thirty other people. You live with these people day after day, month after month, year after year. There are no pubs, no theatres, and few social activities to relieve the monotony. You hear their views ad infinitum, some of which you might not like. You don't have to be within touching distance all the time, but it's difficult to avoid seeing people in such a small space. And every one of these people does something which is ageless, as natural as breathing and as difficult to stop as the passing of time. They all, without exception, gossip. People have tried to stamp it out but it's like trying to prevent human beings from making war or love. You have to live with the certain fact that somewhere on the island, each and every day, your name is cropping up in someone's coversation, and it's likely that they're not forming a fan club for you.

You can do one of two things: you can accept the situation as it stands and decide how much it bothers you. If, on examination, you decide that you can get on with your life without falling apart at the seams because you don't see eye to eye with some other member of the community, then you stay. But if it all becomes too intolerable, then the only alternative is to get out. Everyone falls victim to a bout of paranoia from time to time. The secret is not to let it colour one's view about everything.

I once read a story about a medieval German village. The village lay in a valley and during the winter months access and egress were impossible because of snow on the high mountains surrounding it. A handful of people were thrown together for six months of unrelieved monotony. As soon as the snow melted and the first crocus peeped through, the men took their weapons, marched out of the village and across the mountains to fight it out with the people in a village on the other side. The battle over, they returned and settled down to the peaceful pursuits of farming and family life. A travelling merchant once asked, "Why did this happen?" A thoughtful peasant gave this reply: "For six months I live in the same house with my wife, my children, my parents and my wife's relatives. At the end of the winter I hate them all so much that I would like to kill them. But if I did, life in the village would be impossible. So I go with the men and we fight. Afterwards we all feel much better."

Perhaps this wouldn't be the answer to the problems of any small community, but I do feel that the peasant had as good a grip on the realities of psychology and people's most basic and savage emotions as many a twentieth century idealist. One has to accept certain facts about life in any small community. If there cannot be acceptance there cannot be a strong community.

Egilsay is in a precarious position as far as basic amenities go, and because of the huge turnover in population we are asking questions about the very survival of the community. Recently we had a visit from a prospective councillor and we all asked the question, "Why do we have so little?" An important reason put forward was that we had never had strong representation of our views to the Orkney Islands Council, and the weak link had been our councillor. Perhaps. But a more important and less savoury truth is that we have allowed ourselves to fall victim to the worst symptoms of the island disease. Petty factions and unproductive paranoia have torn us apart and prevented the formation of a strong community. In order to form a cohesive force we must accept that while we cannot tolerate somebody's presence or views in our own home, we must not let these very basic human emotions prevent us from acting as one body in the fight for basic amenities and human rights.

So the disease has its serious as well as its amusing implications. I hope in the future to see its path halted, if not its total eradication.

Chapter 4
If it weren't for the people...

Once in a while a chance remark encapsulates some elusive, fleeting idea and gives it colour and expression. One such remark was made to me by a newcomer to the island who was feeling particularly dejected about his lot. "If it weren't for the people, Egilsay would be a wonderful place." I don't know whether I agree wholly with the sentiment, for it's true that people, despite their shortcomings, can give a place life and character. But at the same time Egilsay has a wild and captivating beauty which has remained unchanged by the passage of time and the activities of its inhabitants.

There are no trees on the island, and this doesn't suit everyone. I don't mind because I've always loved wild, lonely places, and Egilsay is perfection. Her plant and wild life are prolific. There are reputed to be over three hundred different varieties of wild plants and flowers and scores of different species of birds. I'm not a naturalist, but from the aesthetic standpoint alone I can appreciate the island's natural advantages.

Apart from the lack of trees we have it all—pasture, heather-covered hills, lochs, sand dunes, rocky cliffs and a spectacular sea-scape. Egilsay is a place of deep and profound contrasts. One moment the sky is blue, the island basking in the warmth of the sun, bird song fills the air and then, in the space of an hour, a fierce gale will be battering any plants which dare to raise their heads, and horizontal hail and rain will pound the tiny windows of the long, low houses. It is this very capriciousness which gives Egilsay its unique character. Seasons mean very little here. Orkney weather is a law unto itself and refuses to be dictated to by meteorological offices and BBC weather men. Television forecasters tend to point vaguely north and shrug their shoulders despairingly.

In order to survive economically in farming here, one must be better than the best. There isn't a month or even a week when we can be sure of getting in the hay, oats or tatties. Sometimes the weather is so severe that I begin to wonder if humans were ever intended to be here at all. Apart from exploiting the soil, people have done little for the place.

We too are guilty of grandiose schemes for despoiling the island. My husband has nursed many ideas for commercial enterprises of one kind or another, usually involving people. But I have never been an aficionado of these plans, the reason being that I'm not too keen on people, or at least people in such close proximity. I came here to get away from them, and to have them for breakfast, lunch, dinner and all the time in between seems a very refined exercise in sado-masochism. But natural forces work hand in hand with me, and when the idea becomes more than tentative, Mother Nature thrusts so much work upon us that we can think of little else but the tasks in hand, and when the stage of summoning architects and planners is reached the weather flows up and the boat cannot cross. Nature's timing is at its most stunning on an island. She sorts the strong from the puny, the sincere from the insincere, and deals a death blow to all but the most prudent. It's rather like being a raw recruit under a pig of a sergeant major. You hate him, respect him, despise him and admire him all at the same time. He makes you slave and sweat and tax yourself to the limit but at the end of the training period you're fit, alert, resourceful and strong enough to accept any challenge. Egilsay will do this for people if they will let her. If you yield and are willing to learn she will change your life for the better. She will offer a gift of incalculable worth, the gift of oneness with earth's natural forces. But you cannot balk or get cocky. If you don't tie your chicken house down she will summon up a gale and sweep it away. If you go to town when the weather is right for haymaking a month of rain will follow which will rot the crop.

In the long run people have made little difference to Egilsay, while she has made a vast difference to their lives. Island life, with its strange and tenuous mixture of isolation from the intense involvement with other human beings, has a lasting effect upon everyone. A person may imagine that they can come here, stay for a while, and leave unchanged. This isn't so. When you step from the boat onto the shores of this or any other island you are at the beginning of an affair. The affair may involve love and a lasting union or hatred and despair. Egilsay will turn you inside out so that your true self is revealed. That self, the inner being, might be that for which you have been searching, but it could just as easily be the truth from which you would prefer to hide.

Chapter 5
Breaking new ground

We came to Egilsay as the very first English settlers; new, fresh and very naive. To the old-timers we were quite a novelty with our menagerie and strange ideas about what to grow and where to grow it. The natives, though very friendly, treated us with a kind of bemused contempt.

Many had never eaten weird vegetables like radishes and celery and looked on in amazement as we transplanted seedlings outside—in Orkney! They shook their heads and said, "You'll never do it." Our goats too were a constant source of amusement, and when we decided to outwinter livestock, plough a certain piece of land, build a house, heads shook all around. Well, after five years we still don't know who was right or wrong. No one knew the answers about what was right for us, only our experience could point the way.

To a large extent we were the ambassadors for the English farmers who were to follow us. We did indeed break new ground in many ways and we learned from our mistakes. We allowed ourselves to be influenced and manipulated into doing things which weren't really right. We allowed far too much island interference in the running of our day-to-day lives, but like anyone who jumps headfirst into a lake, we clung to whatever was available.

In small communities, as in all other walks of life, the will of the strong dominates. We were without doubt the weak. We came to a small acreage, the smallest on the island, and we were vulnerable. We were informed that everyone joins in this or that group, everyone goes to social functions on Egilsay, and believed the biggest myth of all, that of shared labour.

In many ways a totally false picture of island life was painted for us. We actually believed that the inhabitants of Egilsay, past and present, threw themselves wholly into the care of their fellow islanders, that it had been a paradise of rural activity where the inhabitants spent long halcyon days toiling in each other's fields. Well they didn't and it wasn't, the reason being that humans on Egilsay are like humans in any other part of the universe. On all but a few isolated occasions such as war, disaster and famine, they, like all of us, were motivated by self interest. Although somebody might help their neighbour up to a point, when it came to a conflict between their own interests and those of their neighbour, the former took precedence every time.

For a long while we participated in the game, and may even have helped to perpetuate the myth for a time. We tried to ignore the fact that there were fundamental and divisive conflicts just below the surface of human relationships, and of course our coming caused a stir and a ripple, and with the arrival of more incomers the ripple grew into a whirlpool, then a maelstrom. For the first time for many years the native inhabitants were compelled to look at themselves honestly, and all but a few had to admit that the community on Egilsay was like any other small community in any part of the world—a mixture of good, bad and indifferent.

I believe that because of this lack of honesty and self-examination in the past, many of the advantages and improvements which came to other Orkney islands completely bypassed Egilsay. While other communities were taking a long hard inward look and deciding that while they didn't necessarily see eye to eye about everything, they could at times form a vanguard in the march toward the future and better things, petty factions and jealousies on Egilsay prevented cohesive action. Thus in 1980 we are still without mains electricity, water, transport and community facilities.

It is difficult to distinguish where total honesty merges into pessimism. I don't want to be pessimistic. I am hard on Egilsay because I care about her future and want to remain here. But I do want to see improvements, and a better life for my children if they decide to stay. I apologise to the old inhabitants. They can accuse me, if they will, of a lack of understanding and a disregard for their traditions. I do not disregard their traditions; I revere them. I have tried to record the very best of Egisay's heritage, and it has had a fine one. But there comes a time when certain myths must be buried and suitably mourned, and we must march onward. The tradition of island independence is a fine one and a noble one, but there comes a point when it is sheer stupidity to soldier on without some of the services which the rest of the country considers essential.

So, unwittingly, we caused a stir here. There was no going back for us or the island, and it was never quite the same as that first year when we looked admiringly upon a relic of the past. At that time I thought we had stumbled upon a unique band of folk, but the longer I stayed here the more I saw that human beings, for the most part, are depressingly similar. Their knowledge and skills may lie in different areas and they may have divergent interests and prejudices, yet all but a few are painfully predictable. Of course Egilsay has had its share of memorable characters, including a few in my time here. Island folklore points to a few larger-than-life men and women, and I wonder why they were any different. The reason is, I suspect, that they were flexible, and permitted the way of life, the environment, the spirit of Egilsay to fashion and sculpture their lives and minds. They knew the secret of a peaceful truce with island life. People tend to come here to change Egilsay, not to be changed by the place. Invariably they fail and sink without trace into the grey mass of nondescript and characterless folk who come and go, making little impact on this wild and beautiful island.

Chapter 6
How much self-sufficiency?

I mentioned self-sufficiency earlier, and it may have been a rather scathing reference. Total self-sufficiency is not possible here, not even by the most expert practitioner of the art in even the best of years. I wonder in fact how much self-sufficiency is possible anywhere, for the term covers so many aspects of life, not just food production.

The climate in Orkney is terrible, especially for the self supporter. There is too much wind, too much rain, too much darkness, and for the best part of the year too much cold for anything to grow. When we do get sun and light it comes in a mad spurt in the month of June. Then the plants and weeds have a crazy race against one another and usually settle for a photo finish. The secret is to get one's seeds in the ground at exactly the right minute so that they can germinate and get a head start on the weeds, but at the right planting time it is usually cold and wet, so the seeds go in late and never make the progress they should.

During our first three years here we had exceptional weather—exceptional for Orkney that is—and so we had excellent crops of most root vegetables, enough to make our freezer bulge at the seams. Our greenhouse yielded hundred weights of delicious tomatoes and cucumbers all grown from seed. The seeds were nurtured by Jan on the window ledge of our living room. I often grumbled when the basins and biscuit tins, full of plastic seed bags, crept right out into the middle of the room, but when I bit into the hard sweet tomatoes, the fruit of his labours, I agreed that it had all been worthwhile.

But 1974 to 1977 were not really representative years. 1978 and 1979 have been appalling. We were lucky to retrieve a few boxes of turnips, potatoes and carrots from a huge growing area.

Everything went wrong. Spring was cold and wet and so was summer. Of course we had the long light days of June, but they were cold wet days. The only vegetarian which forged ahead was the weedy variety. The peas and beans that managed to germinate, indeed anything which stood more that six inches above the ground, was battered by north and west winds. In September 1978 we had a hurricane which laid waste anything which hadn't been retrieved from the garden.

Saturday September 9th started out like any other day. The weather was dull, overcast and a little breezy. For days Jan had been talking of building a barricade in front of one particularly exposed section of the house, facing directly on to the west shore. In the end we gave in and helped him to mix cement and get wooden posts, grumbling as we worked about his paranoia on the subject of 'weather'. "It will come," he kept telling us; "You think I'm crazy but we're going to get one hell of a blast soon!" We laughed. By four in the afternoon we weren't laughing. We were trying to fasten slats of wood across a window frame which threatened to blow in at any time. The winds reached 120 mph, and there was quite a bit of damage around Orkney and Shetland. Now I don't make jokes about the weather, for I know that gales can come at any time of the year, and anyone who doesn't take the necessary precautions is crazy.

I am told that 1978 was not a representative year either, so I must conclude that typical Orkney weather lies somewhere between the good summers of 1974 to 1977 and the lousy one of 1978. Working on this assumption I would say that it is possible to produce enough root vegetables and brassicas to last throughout the year, and a good supply of legumes such as peas and broad beans. Runner beans don't grow on Egilsay—for anyone—and the more exotic varieties of vegetables such as sweetcorn and aubergine are out of the question unless one can afford a large, well-heated greenhouse in which to grow them. A small greenhouse—ours is unheated— is essential for a good supply of tomatoes. We usually buy in onions. We manage to produce some, but the climate is such that they don't get a chance to dry out, and end up in pickling vinegar. In short we don't worry too much about vegetables.

Nor do we concern ourselves about meat. We tried vegetarianism for a while but we lacked energy all the time, the quick boost which the protein from meat seems to give. We compromised and decided that while we wouldn't buy in meat, we would eat that which was slaughtered and prepared here. We began by buying a caddy—an orphan lamb—and fattening and killing him at ten months old. The meat was tender and delicious and surprisingly we ate it without any squeamishness. We were told all kinds of rubbish about needing to be an expert to joint meat. Naturally it's in the best interests of the butcher to perpetuate this myth, but it's just not true. It seemed to us fairly obvious where the various cuts were, and the same applied to the pig and the cow—though on a much, much larger scale. We cure sheepskins and hides, and all manner of things can be made from them—rugs, moccasins, mitts, bags and boots. We have various methods of curing depending on the skin and the weather. Sometimes we use formic acid or alum, especially in damp weather, but when it's fairly warm and dry we cure with a paste made from diesel oil and baking powder. When the skin dries out, again depending on the weather, we go over it with an electric sander. This gives the skin the appearance of suede and makes the skin marvellously supple.

Of all meat producing animals, the sheep must be the most economical. Not only does it fill the deep freeze, but we have a fireside rug to be proud of and enough wool trimmed from the fleece to make several jerseys. I have an Ashford spinning wheel, and while it isn't aesthetically the nicest thing to behold it does the job well enough. My spinning, mostly due to lack of practice, is rather hit and miss, but I've promised myself, when the book is finished, when there are no children around, and the washing, weeding, baking and milking are done, then I shall sit down and persevere until I have several skeins of good evenly spun wool. After that, I shall knit socks, jerseys and mitts for everyone.

The economy of the cow is a little more complicated. With the sheep one seems to be getting a very good deal, but the dairy cow is something else. The average Friesian, Jersey or Ayrshire gives one hell of a lot of milk if she is fed properly, and there hardly seems any point in keeping the animal unless you are going to get the highest possible yield from her. We have always found the regime which a milking animal imposes is a very restricting one, so it comes as a welcome release when we can buy what milk we need for a while from a neighbour and watch someone else drowning in a sea of white liquid, only too glad to get rid of a few pints.

When the cow, or goats for that matter, are in full flow, my whole day revolves around milking, cheese and butter making, and washing buckets and containers. Having a cow is guaranteed to put one off milk and milk products for quite some time. Yet some of my cheeses have been exceptionally good, and have even received praise from experts on the subject. Others were not so good and resembled, well, perhaps best not to say, but biting into a home-made cheese is like setting off on a great adventure, a journey into the unknown. No two are alike. They differ in all sorts of ways—texture, taste and colour. Butter has never been my strong point, but then I have never had a particularly 'creamy' cow or goat, so most of my efforts have been directed towards cheesemaking and trying to get my children to eat endless milk puddings and custards. I dread to think of their poor bodies, soaked in cholesterol.

The time-consuming aspect of self-sufficiency cannot be understood until one attempts to do it. It's impossible for the small nuclear family to accomplish everything. In fact, it would demand a pretty hefty commune to produce everything which modern people need, and modern people need an awful lot! It is not possible or practical to turn the clock back unless one is forced to do so by circumstances of holocaust proportions. People seem unable to live like medieval peasants. We've become accustomed to baths, vacuum cleaners and toilet rolls. We tried hard to forget the last hundred years of progress but it wasn't on, not in Orkney anyway.

So we have learned to compromise. The oil lamps and water carrying lasted for a few months, but we could't wait to get a generator. After six months of singed fingers, aching back muscles, squalour and very little contact with the outside world, I could only echo John Donne's immortal words, "No man is an island."

Apart from the restrictions of climate, Egilsay, more than any other part of Britain, affords one the opportunity to be independent of officialdom and bureaucracy. Because we have so few services we do not suffer interference from the bodies who supply the amenities. The eleven miles of sea between Egilsay and the mainland of Orkney seems to terrify officials of all types. The very hint that they may be stranded here fills them with the kind of dread which only someone facing the prospect of a night with a tribe of cannibals could understand!

But independence is limited. In order to survive we must have money. Our financial survival kit comes by courtesy of the Post Office which we run, and whatever else we can earn from writing and odd jobs. The amount is derisory by today's standards, and it is only because we can produce our own vegetables, eggs and dairy produce that we can survive, and even then our standard of living is very low. We have no car, no labour-saving devices, and we never spend money on pleasures outside the home. Yet despite the drawbacks we have that intangible freedom for which most people strive.

The more I explore the vexed and controversial subject of self-sufficiency, the more I am persuaded that material and physical self-sufficiency can only be achieved when one has developed spiritual and mental self-reliance. Living like this reveals certain truths about oneself which can be alarming. We find that our limitations are pretty severe and that wanting to do something does not necessarily mean that one has the physical or mental capacity to do it.

At first we tried to stretch ourselves in fifty different directions at once, keeping more livestock and cultivating more land than we really needed. We bottled, pickled, froze and stored everything in sight. When I wasn't out collecting dandelions for wine I was down on the beach trying to make salt. We earnestly discussed the possibility of growing enough wheat for flour and wrote off for bee-keeping catalogues. But common sense and a little experience saved us from biting off far more than we could chew. We sat down and examined our situation and decided that to devote time and effort to beekeeping, again in a climate like this, was ridiculous. One of the main drawbacks of living on Egilsay is that excess produce cannot be sold easily. Wheeling and dealing are definitely out!

The main contradiction of island life is that while many come in search of self-sufficiency, in reality there is less opportunity for self-reliance here than anywhere else. The island community now consists totally of incomers, and while they pay lip service to the ideals of self-reliance the term has often become a euphemism for selfishness. They see group effort and cooperation as unnecessary, unless of course it serves their best interests, and compromise is giving in. There is, I am certain, a kind of honest coming together which lies somewhere between the dishonest myth of rural utopia and the present spirit of total non-cooperation. For the sake of Egilsay and its inhabitants there must be. If there is not, then the island may as well be turned over to sheep, for the survival of its community life isn't worth fighting for. The type of purist self-sufficiency which attracts so many aficionados is totally impossible without the group activity which is often so unattractive to the independent spirits who flock to remote rural communities all over Britain.

Chapter 7

A new peasantry?

Most of the new islanders farm less than a hundred acres. On that amount of land it is an uphill struggle to keep a handful of breeding cattle and their followers. The work involved in caring for and feeding livestock is tremendous, especially in the climate of Orkney.

In Europe the farmer with such a small acreage and number of cattle belongs to the peasant class. I dare say that an Egilsay farmer wouldn't care to be called a peasant, but albeit unwittingly they are very definitely a part of a new peasantry. In many ways the life of the Orkney peasants is ten times as hard as their European counterparts. For a start they are newcomers to the land. They have no traditions, no native culture upon which to draw, and are more often than not faced with massive financial problems. The proceeds of the sale of a medium-sized house and garden in southern England may buy a farm in Orkney, but it certainly won't cover the cost of livestock and machinery. And so the newcomer's physical strength is tested to the limit by un-accustomed and exacting work in an inhospitable climate, while their mental strength is sapped away by the spectre of an ever-increasing overdraft. The constant prayer of the newcomer is, "Please God let me get through the next ten years and then things will be fine!" What a time! Ten Years! How many urbanites who toil in the cities and towns of Britain ever have to look ahead for more than a few days? They think of tomorrow and the next day and beyond that is the great unknown which doesn't concern them. But this is the very nature of peasant life. Ten, twenty, even fifty years are as nothing. This same island with its rich earth and vegetation will still be here in a hundred years' time, barring a nuclear holocaust. One's initiation into the peasant class begins with this acceptance of the basic premise that one is part of a Grand Scheme, an unending cycle of events. There is no beginning. There is no end.

Those who come with the idea of speculation, investment, tax dodging or a peaceful retirement never learn this lesson. They rarely stay and are almost invariably very unhappy here. They wander about, out of tune with the surroundings, looking like heavy-weight wrestlers in the midst of a fine and beautifully coordinated ballet.

One of the most essential things which is missing from the life of most new peasants is, quite simply, discipline—both self-discipline and the other more rigorous type which the land imposes upon you. The peasant's life, though seemingly spent in days of happy and relaxed rustic pleasure, is as neat and well-ordered as the information coming from a finely tuned computer. The peasant knows as much about time control and labour economy as any well-paid and highly organised firm or work study consultants. For centuries we have been tricked into the assumption that 'peasant' is synonomous with 'stupid' or 'witless'—the image of the happy but cretinous buffoon wielding a hoe.

Not so. The successful peasant—the peasant whose family eats—has a high degree of intellect as well as supreme physical stamina and coordination. The most difficult concept of all has been grasped—so alien to most people today—which decrees that we must bend to the will of natural forces. We cannot control them, therefore we must work in accord with them. It seems that only the most intelligent and open-minded can grasp this truth, and we must necessarily assume that the peasant belongs to this elite. That is not to say that the peasant has not been subject to exploitation, hardship and poverty through the ages; but this is no criticism of the peasant mentality, for as we all know, a good intellect is no shield against persecution, violence and cruelty inflicted by those with more power and better finances.

Unfortunately even the peasants themselves have been indoc-trinated with the idea that they are worthless and that their work and life lacks dignity—witness the hundreds and thousands who have left the land for employment in factories and offices. Agricultural policies and economic laws have made certain that there is no longer a place for the peasant in western civilisation. We are given the impression that the peasant is responsible for the ludicrous agricultural policies of the EEC. Scorn is heaped upon the farmer with less than a certain number of cattle or who farms under a certain number of acres, and if they're not mechanised to the hilt they're beneath contempt.

Why can the agricultural policies of the EEC not be fashioned to accommodate the peasant class? Why not draw upon this wealth of expertise and farming knowledge instead of wooing people away from the land to work in factories, where their only real contribution to life is obsolescence? We should be fostering the idea of the decentralisation of huge combines in industry and farming. Of course the idea is unpopular, and many reasons and cliches can be trotted out in support of the counter-argument; but for the sake of the earth's limited and much abused resources we must give the idea of the small farmers with their small operations some credence.

But maybe the tide is turning. We do seem to be at the beginning of a movement back to the land. If we aren't, we might as well dig our graves, for the warning signals have been sounded. Many countries are now having to ration the consumption of oil and petrol. The West is awakening to the dangers of nuclear proliferation, pollution, the abuse of chemicals and drugs, and the other related activities which indicate people's lunacy. The seeds of mistrust in this kind of progress have been sown. There is a growing reverence towards country life, crafts and the ideal of the peasant life; but these concepts are themselves naive. They may provide a useful springboard, but we must accept that there is more to life on the land than a little light work tempered with much philosophising and drinking of home-made wine. We must be prepared for the rigours and discipline of the peasant life.

Egilsay's present and future development would provide a useful and fascinating study for any sociologist. Are we part of a triggering process, albeit unwittingly? Could it be a pattern, a blueprint for other small island communities? Will there be a stable, hard-working community here in the decades to come? Will they develop a rich culture and working traditions of their own, or will Egilsay become a haven for parasites and tax dodgers? It will be interesting to watch developments, but I am hardly an impartial witness with so much already invested in this beautiful island. I hope for the very best but, like all true peasants, I am prepared for the very worst.

Chapter 8
What about the children?

The main drawback of life on Egilsay for those with school-age children is the fact that they must continue their education at twelve on the mainland. For many island families this is the breaking point. I have nightmares about the time when we shall have to face this awful problem.

But on the other hand, some of the very things which make life on Egilsay very difficult and irritating for adults can prove to be advantageous for children. The life of the average suburban or city child is totally divorced from basic forces. It has no idea where the electricity for the television programme comes from. Does it know or care about the source of the water it drinks and the food it eats? Does it have any knowledge or control at all over the environment in which it lives? This cannot be said of young people on Egilsay. From an early age they witness the workings of the generator, they learn to use water sparingly in the summer when the wells dry up, they watch livestock being killed and jointed and know nothing of the highly coloured and neatly wrapped packages of meat which grace the supermarket shelves. Children here are at the source of most of the vital things which influence and shape their lives. They see processes through from beginning to end, a privilege which is denied most children.

But of course the crux of the whole argument is, "What does one want from one's children?" Perhaps it is important that they should develop a veneer of sophistication at an early age, have good table manners, speak correctly and attend a school which prepares them for GCE's, CSE's, or whichever other examination happens to be in fashion. Maybe this is the only way in which they can be equipped for survival in today's world. But, will tomorrow's world be the same? It could be that the future holds some nasty shocks for us. We are using and abusing the earth's resources at an alarming rate, so relentlessly that a major catastrophe is inevitable. We must make an attempt at preparing our young ones for post-catastrophe living. And what a preparation Egilsay offers, for there is very little other than what one provides for oneself. Amenities and services which most children look upon as rightfully theirs are non-existent on Egilsay. A child's imagination and resourcefulness are given full rein. Of course, while this is good grounding for the child it can put a massive strain upon parents. We must be equally imaginative and resourceful in order to guide our children. There are no clubs, sports facilities, cubs, scouts, swimming pools, parks or gymnasia, so if we wish our children to have similar opportunities to the rest of the children in the country we must provide some of these amenities, either on a communal basis or as individual families. We have opted for the latter, and over the past few years we have managed to build all manner of outdoor equipment, including a trampoline, and in and around our home are facilities for table tennis, badminton and other less energetic games. As far as toys go, I should say we have twice as many as the average family, though by toys I do not mean junk, I mean such things as Lego and Meccano, so that our children should not feel totally isolated and deprived. Because they receive very little teaching in sports we must take responsibility for coaching in tennis, table tennis and football. We try to start projects on birds, wildlife—any topic which will draw on Egilsay's rich environment. The idea that country children can be shooed outside and left to play unsupervised with nature's toys all day is a total fallacy. Given the right people with tremendous enthusiasm this can be a children's paradise. But nowhere else can bad parenting become so glaringly obvious. Without parental energy and interest Egilsay can be more of a hell-hole for a child than the worst slum in the dirtiest city.

While parents are the most important people in a child's life, the teacher must come a close second, and this is even more true in an isolated community. Egilsay's school building is a drab and unprepossessing place. It is a relic of Victorian times, when windows were set high so that pupils should not be distracted from their work. The one room is high, dark, and draughty. But it's the singer and not the song which matters, and a good teacher on the island can mean the difference between mediocrity and excellence for the children. The post is a difficult one. It taxes even the very best teacher to the limit. The house is attached to the school. In fact, every aspect of the teacher's life is attached to the school. They must be prepared to take on a way of life rather than just a job of work. They must be an all-rounder in every sense of the word. Their work, not to mention their private life, is under the constant scrutiny of a small and critical community. Short stays are the order of the day. Only the most saintly and even-tempered can sit in such a hot-seat for more than a couple of years. But short stays are not particularly good for young children, for in the early years of school life they need continuity and stability, and it is all too easy for a disturbing pattern to be perpetuated. A teacher arrives, new and fresh to island life, then comes the realisation that this just isn't any old job. And so because of the nature of such a post, the settling-in period is much longer, and this necessarily reflects upon the quality of the teaching. And what of the time when the teacher discovers that island life is not for them? They cannot escape for evenings and weekends. The teacher is on top of the job for twenty-four hours every day for most of the year. Such a post, if the teacher becomes unhappy, can be like a death sentence, and all these conflicting emotions must reflect on the handling of the pupils. A succession of two or three dissatisfied teachers could mean that a child's education is seriously and irreparably impaired.

Things are not too depressing from our point of view because I am a qualified teacher myself and can supplement and even take total responsibility for my children's education if necessary. For the parents who are not teachers and cannot supplement their child's education, the situation is a potentially serious one. On small islands there is a strong case for home education if the parents are competent and capable, and if home education is too final a step to take, why not start some kind of community school? Many of the new inhabitants of Egilsay and similar islands seem to have been involved in educational work, and we have often thought of drawing upon this experience for the benefit of our children. Why stick to rigid and formal patterns of education in isolated communities where this usually involves a one-teacher school with its obvious drawbacks? Personally I do not consider that a one-teacher school is the best place for my children, but of course I must also add that on Egilsay at the moment it is the best alternative, in fact the only alternative to a very sheltered and isolated existence if my three children were educated totally at home. However, I look upon their time in the school, no matter how high the quality of the teaching, as but a small part of their total education. Ideally we work hand-in-hand with the teacher who runs the school, and the relationship can be a rewarding and beneficial one to all concerned.

When one comes to an island, one must be prepared to accept some sort of 'package deal', and that deal includes one's own future and, more importantly, that of one's children. Few people stop to ask the question, "Am I being *really* fair to my kids?" I didn't, for my son was barely two when we first arrived and our two adopted boys were not then with us. Schooldays were a long way off in a very hazy future. Besides, that one-room school with its pleasant teacher and handful of pupils seemed an attractive place. I didn't ask questions such as, "Is it good for my children to be taught by one person for seven years?" "Can one person be expected to provide all the stimulation which my children are going to need?" and "Am I not inflicting a very narrow and limited life and education upon my offspring?"

Now these questions are engraved upon my subconscious, and consequently I have become very education conscious. Each day before and after official school my children do 'school at home'. We carry on through school holidays and on Saturdays and Sundays, and the children seem to thrive on it. We have our own equipment, reading schemes, and related materials and activities. Both my husband and myself are alert to ways of imparting all aspects of basic and general knowledge. We firmly believe that our children have the right to the best of both worlds.

But as this chapter is dedicated to the children, I must leave the final words to them. Recently we were feeling very low and depressed and talked of leaving Egilsay. As with everything, we discuss these matters in front of our kids, believing that they have a right to know how we feel about things. A look of horror passed over my eldest son's face, "Leave Egilsay . . . ." he gasped, "I'm not going, I love it here!" And so he wins yet again!

Perhaps after all it isn't such a bad thing to be able to run free—weather permitting—and walk from the front door onto a beach with craggy rocks which have been fortresses, pirate ships and the basic materials for so many flights of fancy. And it is a joy to see one's children breathing unpolluted air and learning about the natural things of life in such an unpretentious way. Whatever the future holds for them, at least they have known a few years of the kind of uninhibited joy and physical freedom which is denied to many children.

Chapter 9
And the future?

The best one can say of Egilsay's future is that it is uncertain. Optimistically, one would hope for a halt in both depopulation and population movements in general. Pessimistically, if the activities of the past year are anything upon which to base one's judgement, then we are due for a tremendous amount of change and turmoil. In the past year there has been a 75% turnover in the population and the bulk of the people leaving were newcomers, that is, people who had been here for eighteen months or less.

Their reasons for leaving were many and varied—economic, personal and a general feeling that Egisay is very much a Cinderella when it comes to the allotment of money for facilities and resources. But of course it's the old chicken and egg argument. If we don't have a stable community then we have no chance of getting amenities, and if we do not have the amenities then we shall never have a stable population, and the right people will never be attracted to the island. And this is at the very heart of the problem. What kind of people come to a remote island? What kind of people are prepared to come and stay in a place without mains water, electricity and transport? They are certainly not the kind of gregarious folk who are likely to throw themselves wholeheartedly into communal activities, otherwise they would hardly be attracted in the first place. They are, for the most part (and I hope they will forgive me), eccentrics and non-conformists. They are people who have grown dissatisfied with cities and crowded places, those who prefer isolation (or think they do), and those who are notoriously bad at any kind of communal discipline. Other types come as well— the nice, the normal, the cooperative—but they soon find that this is not the place for them. Without doubt the people who stay for any length of time fall into the former category. It's an unsavoury fact but it must be faced.

Various people, myself among them, have refused to face these facts and have tried to whip up enthusiasm for community activity. Most attempts are doomed to failure. It's rather like trying to fashion a neat, conforming shape from a huge amorphous mass; like being a shepherd with a flock of recalcitrant sheep. They refuse to be directed. They will not be organised. They are a group of strong-willed, single-minded people who have no inclination or intention of accepting the disciplines of community life. Meetings usually end up close to civil war without conclusions being drawn or definite plans of action being hammered out. No matter who organises a social function, undoubtedly someone else feels that they could have done it much better. They will not face the fact that each and every community needs a leader. No one will be led, and apart from a few uneasy communal occasions, each family, function or group stays pretty much within its own boundaries.

Territorial rights are another problem. If you have been accustomed to a back garden or even five acres, the acquisition of a hundred acres or more is quite a novelty, and at first you want to flex you muscles. You do silly things like forbidding your neighbours from peacefully crossing your land over which they've had a right of way since time immemorial. You carp about folk using the beach along your foreshore, which in any case is crown-land. And then there are those who go to the other extreme and believe that they have unimpeded access to the whole island. It belongs to them to do with as they will. They may have seen Egilsay just before the natives left, when it looked as if people did what they pleased without any problems. But in reality it wasn't like that at all. There was an unseen but nevertheless rigorous discipline, a strict *modus vivendi,* but because it was unseen it went unnoticed by the newcomer. So we are blighted with those who believe that it doesn't matter if their sheep, cattle and assorted livestock wander unchecked over their neighbour's land. The attitude is, "We are on an island and we can do as we please. It doesn't matter if our dogs roam around the place worrying sheep and annoying people. Who cares? We're on an island. What freedom!"

It sounds like chaos and it is. Of course one expects chaos, unrest and the spilling of blood at the beginning of any revolution, and that is exactly what it is—a revolution. But all revolutions must come to an end, and peace and stability must reign if progress is to take place. There is a great deal at stake. With every internal upheaval and radical population movement, essential services slip further and further away. Outside bodies see the unrest on the island and take full advantage. They work on the assumption that if we have a moving population on Egilsay then it will not be an organised and vociferous one. No one will notice if Egisay's name is moved to the bottom of yet another list for better transport, pier developments, mains water and a new community centre. With each upheaval we lose a little more, our grasp on a better future becomes weaker. This then makes inevitable the departure of those few genuine settlers who have invested much in the island.

Another disturbing development is the lack of families with children. At the moment there are only six children under thirteen, and three of them are mine. There are only two children in the school, and as they both happen to be my children this makes the situation even more serious. We are beginning to question whether it is fair to our children to stay here. I hope that we can hold on and that families with young children will come.

But people must come here with a realistic attitude. This is no place for the 'simple life' or a peaceful retirement. It is a place of hard physical work with few rewards. What one does get in return is a kind of freedom, a kind of peace which one does not get elsewhere; but the price for that peace and freedom is high. To come here dissatisfied in search of an answer to one's personal problems is futile. Dissatisfactions and problems grow in isolation; they rarely diminish. It is of course impossible to make judgements about the type of person best suited to island life. Sometimes the most unlikely people survive here, and those who strike one as admirably equipped soon become disillusioned. Each person who arrives is facing a period of adjustment, an inward journey. If this initial and stressful period can be tolerated and accepted for what it is, then perhaps people will be able to ride the storm and give island life a fair chance. It is during this difficult period that they are most likely to leave. Naturally folk are going to go after periods of ten, fifteen or twenty years, but at least they will have contributed something to community life. People who come and go within two years simply have a parasitic effect. They leave very much 'in the red', heavily overdrawn on the island's bank of goodwill and practical help.

Egilsay's problem is a universal one seen in a microcosmic setting: few are prepared to accept self-discipline and responsibility for their own and maybe even other people's actions, and those who do, have an intolerable burden placed upon them. So much so that inevitably they too will often pack up and leave. And when those who hold the balance between order and chaos also go, then the future will be grim. We must all accept that no one can survive on an island without some cooperation and goodwill.

Apart from a minority of incurable optimists, the general view is that things will not get any better. I try to keep my views in the centre, a mixture of pessimism and optimism, of objectivity and personal feelings. And maybe the optimists are right. Maybe Egilsay's own rigorous selection process will throw up a group of people who can accept the hard work, discipline and ultimately the joys of island life; people who can sink differences, sublimate selfishness for the mututal good. If the people who genuinely care about Egilsay can hold on until this happens, then we may look forward to a brighter future with essential amenities and a thriving community.

Whatever happens, we as a family have gained much of importance during our time here. We have had the opportunity to explore the kind of self-knowledge which is denied most people. Egilsay, apart from being a beautiful and captivating island, is a storehouse of knowledge. Those who are prepared to open their hearts and minds will receive the most priceless gift of all—the ability to know human limitations and accept, with good grace, that which is inevitable.

PART TWO
PAPA STOUR

Vicki Coleman

Chapter 1

How it happened

After eight years I am still unfailingly impressed by the beauty of the island of Papa Stour. I thought on the day that I first landed on the isle that it was a very special place, but with time one sees closer and deeper, and I do not anticipate ever growing tired of it.

Never in the earlier part of my life did I have an inkling that I would find happiness and fulfilment on a small Shetland island; when I consider the fact that I live in a spot so remote, isolated and difficult to get to, I surprise myself even now. There are those who regard people like us as escapists, and accuse us of avoiding the issues of the day, but life cannot be avoided—the pressures are everywhere. Life on Papa Stour is full, demanding, difficult, rewarding, exciting, but never dull and featureless.

I came to Papa Stour by way of a public school in East Anglia, a secretarial course, Rhodesia and 'the road'. It was when I was on the road that my horizons began to widen. Before that I had expected to marry a solicitor, live in a suburb and give dinner parties. On the road, however, the search was on; unconsciously at first, for I didn't know what I was doing there—I just thought I was travelling to yet another place—but everyone I met was looking for something, a new way, a different attitude to life, an adventure. There were always so many ideas, so much to talk about. After my respectable middle-class upbringing I was astonished at the variety of people's attitudes to life based on earlier experiences which were totally different from my own.

After school I did a secretarial course; this was at a technical college, and I found myself at something of a disadvantage socially. I suddenly realised that my education so far had been that which is given only to a privileged minority. I didn't speak like most of the people I met, and it was obvious that my experience had been totally different. This in itself was no disadvantage, but I had no confidence since it seemed that the sum of my experiences so far was nil. I felt that I was regarded with amusement, wariness and slight scorn—I felt out of place.

As the years went by I gained confidence, escaped to London, and eventually moved into a flat full of lovely mad Irish people— they accepted me and I felt more comfortable. I did some secretarial work and became a reporter on a motoring paper. Enthusiasm for cars, and especially old ones, ran in the family; one of my brothers had a historic old racing car. Yet it is with considerable amazement that I look back on this period, since the almost universal noise and fumes of the internal combustion engine have been instrumental in my decision to move to an island with only a mile of road, five tractors, one Land Rover, one motorbike, one cement mixer and a great deal of very fresh air.

My experience as a racing reporter stood me in good stead later. I answered an advertisement in the Personal column of *The Times* for companions for a Land Rover trip to Africa. Ending up in Salisbury, Rhodesia, I was able with my professed skills in journalism to find a job immediately as a reporter with the *Rhodesia Herald*. It could hardly have been a more interesting time; the newsroom was always brimming with excitement, and a few months later independence was declared.

Kevin and I met in Salisbury, and it is unlikely that our paths would have crossed had we remained in England, as I was hemmed in by the class barriers imposed on me by my upbringing and he was a trade union man with left-wing leanings and no particular desire to fraternise with the bourgeoisie.

He is from a working class Leeds family of Irish origin, and spent his first few years in a back-to-back house in the slums of Leeds city centre. When he was eleven they moved to a new council estate on the outskirts of Leeds. His parents both worked hard to provide him, their only child, with a comfortable home. Since the mid 1950s when the estate of neat semi-detached stucco houses was built, the gardens have matured; Kevin's father and many of the neighbours have done wonders with their tiny gardens; their homes are indeed their castles. But there is something inhibiting about this type of environment—a feeling of the state organising the workers.

Kevin began to feel the oppressiveness of it when he was fourteen. He went to an unenlightened secondary modern school where the pupils were regularly reminded that their future role in life was as factory workers. He saw his mates leave and get factory jobs, and the pattern for girls was the family way—they would marry young, live with their parents in difficult and often unhappy circumstances, and eventually get a council box of their own. His reaction was, "There must be more to life than this," and I am thankful for that, as otherwise I should never have met him. Whether it was just luck that he didn't get caught in the early marriage trap, or what it is that makes one odd person in hundreds unwilling to conform we cannot say, but coming to Papa Stour has given us the opportunity to develop as real individuals, and for us to go back now to the type of life we were brought up in would be very, very difficult.

He left school just before his fifteenth birthday, and his father saw to it that he was apprenticed to a trade rather than put to work in a factory. It took five years to complete his apprenticeship as an electrician, but after three years he started getting out-of-town jobs. He was the 'cowboy spark', going for the big money, living in ridiculous conditions, working ghosters (consecutive shifts). Having always lived under his parents' roof with a very motherly Mum he had no knowledge of cooking, and while working on a power station job in Hertfordshire and living in a caravan it was his custom to hardboil three dozen eggs on a Sunday and eat them through the week.

Whilst I arrived in Salisbury by Land Rover having come via the eastern Mediterranean countries, Kevin arrived at almost the same time after hitch-hiking from England via Gibraltar and North Africa. He was travelling with a guitar and not much else and getting occasional work as a folk singer. I thought he was a lovely and sincere singer. He still is, but sadly he doesn't do a lot of singing now; he says his good singing came from those days of suffering . . . on the road, penniless, hungry, confused. After he met me it wasn't really like that any more . . . such are the ironies of life. I was neither penniless nor hungry and willingly shared what I had.

Although we met in Salisbury, at no time did it occur to us to settle down in Africa. We both wanted to go back to England, though we didn't know what we should do once we got there. So we returned to Europe travelling fourth class on a Portuguese boat. I shared a cabin with five other women and a new baby, and Kevin had one with five other men; although mostly married, men and women were segregated, which was difficult as it was a three-week voyage from Durban to Lisbon and naturally enough husbands and wives wanted to be alone with each other from time to time. We all survived however, and continental touches such as wine with every meal even in fourth class helped to compensate.

Back in England we didn't really know what to do with ourselves. Kevin hadn't given up his ambition to go to India; he had been intending to go there on his previous trip abroad but got diverted in Egypt and went south instead of east. After a year or two of drifting rather uncertainly he finally set off again. There was never any question of my accompanying him; although I liked to travel I did not feel the compulsion that he did to go on the road, and he wouldn't have let me go with him anyway. He likes to travel rough because that is where the exciting experiences are, but having to protect this small and delicate 'English rose' out East would have been a monstrous burden.

So we went our separate ways. I got a job in a bookshop on the South Coast and went to live in the country, and Kevin set off for India. He was away for two and a half years, and in that time I received three or four cards from him. I didn't really intend to wait for him, but I was still around when he got back.

When we met again it was as if we had never been apart, and it seemed that his travelling was over for the time being and we could stay together. I knew by then that I wanted to have a child, and it came as a joyful surprise to find that Kevin too had children in mind.

But where should we live and what should we do? I had already been to Scotland and spent a holiday at the Findhorn Community in Morayshire. Shortly after Kevin returned from India we went to Inverness-shire and stayed a week or so with some old friends at their primitive abode above Loch Ness. This clinched it. I was in love with the Scottish scenery, the lochs, the hills, the glens, the bracken and the silver birch trees. But more than that, our friends were living the sort of life that I wanted to live, out in the wilds with freedom to think and grow in spirit, and without the constrictions of the rat race. They were struggling to make a living, but they were happy and fulfilled. Their surroundings were inspiring with the magic mountain of Mealfourvonie behind and the steep forest leading down to Loch Ness in front. Kevin loved it there too, and we both were getting a clearer idea of what we wanted— to break away from the quiet well-regulated life where the best hours of each day were given over to a job that was at best only partially fulfilling.

We sold our cottage in Hampshire, and May 1972 found us in Morocco getting a final warm-up before heading north. June and July were spent with our friends near Loch Ness. Staying with them was like a training period for what was to follow, and we learned a variety of survival techniques. I discovered how to make salads out of chickweed and to eat the tops of the turnip seedlings as we thinned them out. One day whilst returning from the village ascending a steep hill, the fish delivery van in front of us had its doors open and a parcel of fish slid out right at our feet. The van driver was quite oblivious and there was no way we could catch him up, so we had a rare and delicious fish supper that night. We slept in our tent and bathed in the burn—it was a lovely summer. We would have like to have stayed there, but soon found out that although there are many derelict cottages in Scotland, persuading the owners to part with them is downright impossible. They would rather watch them fall to pieces.

Thurso in Caithness beckoned at the end of July—there was a folk festival there and we felt it was time to make a move. The people we met were salmon fishermen on the north coast of Caithness—it is a seasonal occupation but lucrative in a good season, and obviously they enjoyed the large amount of free time that they had and did not immediately rush off to take another job in the intervening months. Friends of theirs—another fisherman, his wife and child—had recently moved to a small island in Shetland called Papa Stour, and the story was that anyone who went there was given a croft and five sheep.

We did not actually believe this, neither did we especially want a croft and five sheep, but we were intrigued. We had planned to go to the Western Isles next but decided as we were already so far north we would divert for a week or so and have a look at Papa Stour. The obvious thing was to get on a boat going from Scrabster, just outside Thurso, to Orkney, and thence we thought to Shetland. This turned out to be a mistake, and just showed our ignorance of sea travel; with the sea, the shortest distance between two points is rarely the right route to take. We stood on the cliffs above Thurso and could see the Old Man of Hoy and were told that that was Orkney, so we bought tickets on the steamer *St. Ola* going to Stromness the following afternoon. I have since heard a lot about the Pentland Firth and how rough it is, and it lived up to its reputation that day by giving us an uncomfortable few hours. It came as a complete surprise to us on arriving in Stromness to be told that boats rarely run from Orkney to Shetland and the orthodox way of getting there from the Scottish mainland was an overnight steamer trip from Aberdeen. So we hitchhikers ended up having to fly from Kirkwall in Orkney to Sumburgh in Shetland.

The hottest night I have ever spent was in a barn near Kirkwall Airport. We slept on a mound of newly made hay, comfortable, deliciously sweet-smelling, but so hot. While we were in Kirkwall Airport the following day a Danish plane landed with passengers en route to the Faroe Islands. Orkney and Shetland have strong links with Scandinavia, and it was at this point that I began to realise that the history and culture of the Northern Isles differs considerably from that of the rest of the British Isles.

From Sumburgh at the south end of the mainland we caught a bus to Lerwick, Shetland's one and only town, and another out to Sandness on the west side, where we were told we would be able to get a boat to Papa Stour.

The road from Walls to Sandness is one of the most extraordinary roads I have ever seen. It winds, and winds, and winds. There are no houses at all—only lochs, burns and brown peat moors. To see a human being on this road is a rare event. That evening I thought it was incredibly gloomy, but I find now that I have tuned into the special attractions of the Shetland landscape I always enjoy its wild expanse. After eight miles of winding you come to the top of a hill and there before you is the sea, and in the distance to the west the green isle of Papa Stour. What a joy it is now to come over the top of Sandness Hill, to glimpse Papa again and know that I will soon be home.

It was a Friday evening, and not knowing what we were looking for it took us some time to locate the pier. We had arrived at the pier head just in time to see a small boat several hundred yards away, and heading out across the sound. We felt helpless and dashed as we stood stranded at the end of that long and winding road. We pitched our tent in the garden of the unoccupied laird's house at Melby, just above the pier, and settled down for the night. Nobody seemed to know when the next boat would be. Officially there was—and still is—a mailrun on Monday, Wednesday and Friday mornings at nine o'clock, but we found out very soon that things don't really work the official way on Papa Stour. On Saturday afternoon the boat came again and unloaded a swarm of summer visitors who had been staying on the island. We went aboard and headed for the island. It was a fine bright sunny day with a stiff breeze and a blue sea; spray came over the bows of the *Venture* as we headed across Papa Sound. The island lay like a green jewel before us, the white crofthouses looking neat and well cared for.

By this time, I was distinctly nervous. I felt as if I were going to a private place where I had no business to be. Yet Kevin remembers the day he first stepped onto Papa Stour as a time when a great weight lifted off him. I was suffering from paranoia.

As it turned out, we were stepping onto an island in turmoil. There were at the time sixteen Shetlanders living on Papa Stour and things were becoming more and more difficult for them; a chronic lack of manpower is a problem in a place where many of the jobs that are services on the mainland—such as water supply and the electricity—have here to be maintained by the islanders themselves. But the main cause of the turmoil was that in the previous six months five couples plus five children, and including three expectant mothers, had arrived with the intention of settling on the island with no more than the vaguest idea of what was involved and a leaning towards 'alternative living'. Three of the families were English and two Scottish. In six months the population of this quiet island had doubled.

A few days after our arrival there was an unprecedented event in the history of crofting. A Hearing was held in the then disused schoolroom for the purpose of determining whether three crofters who had apparently left the island should be dispossessed of their crofts in the light of the crucial population situation, thus clearing the way for newcomers to apply for the tenancy of these crofts. According to crofting law a crofter must live within ten miles of his holding. Many families had left Papa Stour, and when we arrived on the isle others were making plans to leave. In the case of one of the crofts in question sheep were still on it, and the crofter, who had moved to the mainland, visited the isle only at lambing time and on other rare occasions. This was quite obviously a poor state of affairs, as the stock had so little supervision, yet their owner was able to claim the government subsidy for hill sheep. The Court decided that two of the absentee crofters should be dispossessed, and these two crofts did eventually become tenanted by newcomers.

It amazes me now that we had so little idea of what we wanted to do. We were attracted to the idea of living on Papa Stour; we quickly made friends with some of the other incomers, and found we had quite a lot in common. This was before John Seymour published his famous book on self-sufficiency, but we were thinking along those lines. We did believe that home-grown vegetables grown with good old muck were nicer and better for you than the mass-produced ones that had been drenched in pesticides and shot up with chemical fertilisers. We viewed the state of the world and we questioned everything—the government, the law, defence policy, and especially our materialistic consumer society, and we found a great deal wanting. It was not for us to change it; we couldn't; but it was for us to show by living in a different way that there were other possibilities. We would try and do as little harm as possible to our planet and to our neighbours.

Our plans as far as they went had been to find a house probably in a semi-ruinous condition in a remote but very beautiful part of Scotland, to live there, do up the house and work a small piece of land, and support ourselves by getting work in the neighbourhood. But the problem with Papa Stour and other small islands is that there is absolutely no chance of employment in the neighbourhood. We had a little money to be going on with, and when friends offered us a caravan of sorts for the winter we accepted joyfully. Still playing it by ear we assumed that a way to earn a living would manifest itself before long.

The longer I stay on Papa Stour the more I love it, and the more beautiful I think it is. We do like the isolation. We spent the first few weeks in walking and talking to our new friends. We were all bursting with ideas—many of them quite impractical. I remember somebody even got the Ministry of Agriculture man to come out to the island to talk about growing brown rice.

Although we had come to see about 'a croft and five sheep', we had no real ambition to be crofters. Neither of us knew much about farming and I had every intention of having several babies within the next few years. Neither did it take us long to find out that crofts weren't actually being given away.

However, an alternative livelihood did manifest itself in the form of a shell-fishing boat. Another newcomer to the island had obtained a grant and loan for a boat from the Highlands and Islands Development Board, and Kevin agreed to crew for him. The Highland Board, as its name implies, exists to assist industry and enterprise in the Highlands and the western and northern Scottish islands. Some of the schemes they support are on a very big scale, and although our fishing boat must have been a minor project for them, to us it seemed that we were borrowing an enormous amount of money. It appeared to be a good opportunity for us to establish ourselves, but I imagine some of the old-timers on the isle must have been shaking their heads over our innocence of the sea and its ways. I certainly had no idea of what Kevin was in for—the long hours at sea in a small boat in all weathers, the blisters, the rope burns, the hard physical work, the dangers, the narrow escapes. The sea, and especially the sea around Shetland, must never be taken lightly; it is another element. As the years go by and I watch it through the seasons and hear the countless stories of wrecks, salvages, loss of lives and boats, a shudder comes over me at the completeness of my ignorance. Kevin's boating experience up to then consisted of a paddle boat on Roundhay Pond in Leeds; but in fact he turned out to have a good aptitude for the sea, and quickly learned how to handle boats. Thanks to the Boy Scouts he was already competent at knots and splices.

So the boat was ordered, and she was to be built in Orkney. She would be twenty-six foot long and very beamy with a transom stern to allow plenty of room for stacking creels. They were going to fish for crabs and lobsters. We had decided to live on an island.

Chapter 2

The island of Papa Stour

Papa Stour measures about two miles by three, but the coastline is very indented with long inlets, which means that at certain points one may walk from the sea on the south side to the sea on the north side in ten minutes. The small inlets are called geos, the larger ones where boats can anchor are voes. We were camped in a byre to begin with, and although it provided a far better shelter than our tent it was rather dark and we didn't choose to spend many of the daylight hours in there. It looked out onto Housa Voe at the north-east corner of the island, and to open the door on a fine morning was to see the sun rising through the line of stacks that runs from the mouth of the voe on the south side. There was a sea-stack with a hole in it that the golden sun would shine through, though the top of this stack has since been broken off by the pounding seas in a gale, and it is no longer quite as spectacular as it was. We arrived in August and the islanders were trying to make hay, but the weather was unfavourable and it rained a lot. We took to going barefoot as our hiking boots were permanently sodden from the wet grass. After two or three weeks I made a dash into Lerwick and bought two pairs of wellingtons.

Every variety of maritime scenery is here: sandy beaches warmed by the sun at low tide; rock pools full of sea anemones, different sorts of weed and shellfish. There are geos with cliffs on three sides a hundred feet high, vertical sides dropping straight into a deep peacock-blue sea. The cliffs have their ledges jampacked with sea birds, nesting, squabbling, flying off, soaring into the blue sky, diving into the blue sea, always coming back to roost in their avian slum. Offshore there are rocks, holms and stacks of superb grandeur, always impressive but never more so than when a westerly gale is blowing and the sea is churning and boiling around them, obliterating them in white spray and sending thick clouds of spin-drift over the land.

In contrast are the still summer nights when the township of Sandness is bathed in sunlight shining from the north-west, and the Sound is like a mirror with not a ripple in it. We can hear the voices of the Sandness folk and their dogs, and occasionally the whine of an outboard motor as someone goes off for an evening's fishing. When I see it like this it is hard to credit the existence of the fierce winter storms, when huge white breakers roll through the Sound and crash onto the holms of Forewick and Melby that lie in their path.

Inland there are lochs where the red-throated diver nests, and where in winter the huge whooper swans which breed in Iceland come down to feed. And in addition to these wonders, wherever you walk in Papa Stour there are signs of man's habitations of long ago. These date back to the Stone Age, though little is known of how these people existed. There is a great deal of interesting work to be done here in the archaeological field. Excavations are in progress on the island to uncover a mediaeval Norse farmstead, which it is thought might possibly have been the farm of a Norwegian prince. In Viking times an island had advantages as a dwelling place. It was easier to defend; raiders could be spotted when they were some considerable distance away at sea and preparations could be made.

It must have been a life of extreme hardship, because although the land is fertile they could never have had more than a minimum of fuel; warm fires to sit by of an evening just could not have been contemplated by the poorer households, and in our long damp winters life without a fire would have been gloomy to say the least. Papa once had a quantity of poor quality peat, but over the centuries so much of it has been removed that the face of the earth has been scalped, and there is now virtually no soil at all, let alone turf. At the excavations for the Norse farmstead a fireplace has been uncovered, and is thought that seaweed was burned there. Dried seaweed burns quickly, and although much is washed ashore, hauling it up and drying it in quantity would demand a considerable amount of labour, so it is unlikely that it was used other than for cooking.

All the inhabited houses are situated on the east side of the isle where the land is good; here there are also many derelict houses, roofless shells, reminders of days gone by when there were fish-curing stations here and the island supported more than three hundred people. This was in the nineteenth century before ice and refrigeration, and consequently the fishing stations had to be as close as possible to the fishing grounds. In the 1820s there were 36 boats fishing out of Papa Stour. There are ruins of quite extensive buildings at Culla Voe, Hamna Voe and West Voe; at the two former they gutted and prepared ling and cod, these being the most valuable species. After steeping in salt to pickle them, the fish were laid out to dry on the rocks and stones of the beach, and subsequently shipped out in smacks to Europe, chiefly to Spain. A building at North House now used as a tractor shed was then a dried fish store owned by the local merchants, Hay and Ogilvy.

Later the herring fishing came to Papa Stour, and a herring station was built in West Voe. It is hard to imagine now all the hustle and bustle that centred on this trade, with the fishing boats coming in and out to land their catches, and the workers going down to the gutting sheds when a boat came in, other boats arriving with empty barrels to be filled with the small silver fish, packed in rough rock salt and taken off to ports in Europe.

Life must seem sadly changed and quiet now to the old folk who remain on Papa Stour. Whilst they cannot remember those days, they will have heard their parents speak of them. They have watched the population dwindle to almost nothing, and before the incomers arrived in 1972 there were no children living on the island, only occasional summer visits from grandchildren, nephews and nieces. It is a sad community that has no children in it.

Papa Stour, being on the west side of Shetland, is exposed to the Atlantic Ocean, and the wind never allows us to forget it. It is the wind that whips the sea up into a boiling turmoil isolating us from all the world. The way of life demands certain inner resources and a total commitment to the island. There are a few brief weeks in summer when we can leave the island and return the same day, but if we have to go to the town in the winter it may be up to two weeks before we can return. The frustration of waiting for the weather to moderate so we can get home is at times almost unbearable. You cannot even use the time on the mainland profitably as you must remain close to a telephone in case the sea goes down and the boatmen decide to make a dash to Sandness at short notice.

Once, after spending a week's holiday in Scalloway on the mainland in early spring with the whole family, we spent a second week waiting to get home. When it was finally judged safe for the boat to cross, we tidied up the house we had been staying in and called a taxi to take us to Sandness. The taxi driver was half an hour late and we got to the Sandness pier in time to see the *Venture* some distance out and heading for Papa. It was a bad day: the sea was coming over the Sandness pier and threatening to swamp the boat, and there was a stong wind. They had waited as long as they dared.

During the winter we get days and days of wind and driving rain. The smaller children are confined to the house; for them, to go out is to get blown over. I have a picture in my mind of our daughter Chandra, aged about two; she had set off to walk round the end of the house, but there was a westerly gale blowing and as she reached the south end of the house she was met by a violent gust of wind. I came upon her with her arms out, going round and round like a whirling dervish. Eventually she toppled over a bank and rolled down to the bottom where she was in the lee. If they do go out in this weather they cannot be allowed to go far; the shore is not safe as huge waves can come rolling up an empty beach and a child with its mind on other things could easily be swept away.

Although the mailboat is scheduled to cross to Sandness three times a week, during the winter it frequently cannot do so. There are many weeks when they only get across once for mail and supplies, and since we came to the island the longest we have been isolated is sixteen days. In the months of November and December it often seems like Christmas once a week as the extra mail begins to build up. People start to order special supplies and Christmas presents from Lerwick, and in addition to the usual shop stores, mail bags and fodder, there are exciting-looking packages and boxes, even an odd Christmas tree; then come cases of beer and stronger stuff; someone has even ordered a case of wine from a wine club— two bottles broken there on its long journey. In winter the boat day is the signal for a rush of activities. First we must dash to the post office to post our letters and cards; if we miss the post it could easily be a week before there is another chance. Several people usually go on the boat in addition to the crew; it's good to have an extra hand in rough weather, and help is needed to load the accumulated stores. Everyone who is able is expected to go and load their own goods at Sandness if they are heavy—animal feed, gas cylinders or barrels of fuel. Someone might have a new ram to bring in, and phone calls fly to and fro as instructions are given for the beast to be brought to the pier. Many of us also get supplies from the Sandness shop—goods that our own small grocery does not keep. The shopkeeper there, between phone calls from Papa residents, is busy tying up boxes and putting them into his van ready to take down to the pier. When the boat gets in, one or two people will walk the quarter mile up to the shop festooned with empty cans for paraffin and petrol, neither of which is sold on the island, and these will be filled and brought down in the van with the parcels. Sometimes if the sea is running into Sandness and they cannot safely lie alongside, they will just grab the mailbags and perishables and pull out, leaving the bulk of the stores for a better day.

Because of the inadequacies of the Sandness pier—it is too short and was built beside a shifting sandbank—the boat can only tie up for two hours either side of high water. In winter this presents great problems and dangers, as high water may not come within the few hours of daylight that we have.

So the winter is quiet except on boat days, and the summer is feverishly busy. It is not uncommon to see people out hoeing turnips on their rigs or weeding their gardens at ten or eleven o'clock at night. The sun literally seems to give us energy, whilst in winter the generators, which provide most of the houses with electricity, go on at four o'clock and, apart from a trip to the byre to feed the animals or milk the cow, nobody is abroad again till the following morning.

All exterior building work has to be done in the summer; anyone who has tried to erect anything in a gale will be aware of the problems. Reroofing our byre took two summers—one for the south side and one for the north. We used ten-foot sheets of corrugated asbestos, and even a slight breeze meant that they were quite unmanageable when climbing up a ladder and trying to put them into place. Completely windless days are rare and very precious. Many of the houses have felted roofs which need to be tarred every year, and a still summer day will often find an islander up on the roof taking advantage of the weather to get this messy job done.

Some of the islanders have small boats; these are ashore for eight months of the year, but in summer any calm evening will see the

Papa fleet in the Sound fishing for small saithe, known here as piltocks. Others go off with a few creels and come home with crabs and the occasional lobster.

We tend to take it easier in the winter, knowing that the summer will be hectic however well organised we are. Because of the communications problem, visitors all tend to converge on us in the summer; winter visitors are rare and may have to stay longer than they bargained for.

We get a certain amount of amusement from observing how visitors react to the prospect of being storm-stayed on Papa Stour. As far as Council officials and their like are concerned, they prefer to pick the finest of fine days and get an assurance from the boatman that he will be able to make a second crossing to take them back to the mainland. They seem fearful of having to spend a night on the isle, as if we might turn into a tribe of cannibals as darkness fell. This means they are able to put only part of their attention on the problems they have come to see about, since they are concerned about the time at which they have to catch the boat back to Sandness, and how long they should allow to get to the pier.

I often think it would be beneficial for some of these people to spend a night on the isle and see how hospitable we can be. In such a small community it is always a pleasure to have a stranger amongst us for a day or two; someone from a different walk of life can be stimulating for us, and it might also be an interesting and salutory experience for them.

We had a visit not long ago from a photographer and reporter from a Sunday paper. They arranged to stay two days but eventually stayed for five as a bad storm blew up. They had never seen anything like it; there was a terrific sea and they went out and took pictures of it. Apart from those who live in the islands and exposed maritime places, not many people have the opportunity to experience a gale like this, and it is profoundly impressive. Anyone who is under the impression that the human race is in control of this planet will have that idea blown out of his or her head very quickly. We are helpless in the face of the elements.

Chapter 3
My dwellings

Somewhat to the alarm of the crofter who offered it to us, we spent two months in our byre overlooking the stacks, before moving on to better things in the shape of a twelve-by-six wooden workmen's caravan. We had arrived feeling perfectly self-sufficient with our two-person nylon tent, but when a kindly islander offered us a real roof over our heads for the duration of our stay—at that time thought to be about a week—we accepted gratefully. We had no idea of how the Shetland weather differed from that in England or Scotland; but we soon found that it was very windy and, that summer anyway, very wet. If we had had to stay in our tent we would probably have left the island after a couple of days.

Although the roof leaked, the byre had a dry patch where the bed—a series of planks—was, and enough space for us to set up quite a decent temporary dwelling. We had our primus stove, water was obtained from the adjoining house, and fish was plentiful. I can see them now hanging up in the end of the byre during the night, with the phosphorescence gleaming.

The people we had come to see were living in the workmen's caravan, but were in the process of renovating a small but-and-ben—a two-roomed cottage in which the but is the living space and the ben used as a bedroom. Their house was a pretty little cottage, but very delapidated and damp. They had been told they could do it up and live in it; it didn't actually change hands in the legal sense, and when they left, it reverted to its original owners and has not been lived in since. It was thanks to them that we moved into the caravan in October, when life in the byre was becoming rather difficult.

Sad to say there are no less than six houses on Papa Stour that were empty in 1972, have been lived in since and now stand empty again. These are the houses of the people who have come and gone again. Reasons for departure vary; in the main I think it must be the desire to earn more than one can here and so have a better standard of living, and secondly to find more outside stimulation than such a small and isolated community can offer. Unfortunately, whenever someone leaves everyone who remains feels very depressed and saddened; we miss the everyday signs of life—the light in the window, the smoke from the lum, the people coming and going.

Our friends had bought the workmen's hut from an Inverness scrapyard and fitted it out themselves. Gavin did the carpentry, maintenance work and driving; Trisha was expecting her second baby. Matthew was a blithe blond-haired child of sixteen months, and there were four Rhode Island hens who lived contentedly in a box underneath between the wheels. After fitting out was complete they set off for Aberdeen towing the van behind a tractor. Progress was slow but they had all they needed with them including fresh eggs. The whole outfit was put aboard the North Isles steamer and safely disembarked at Lerwick. After towing the van to Sandness, Gavin exchanged the tractor for a boat, and they all went over to the island leaving their home for the time being on the mainland side of the Sound.

Gavin and Trisha were more folk who could not fit into the backgrounds in which they had been raised. They had chosen to live rough in Caithness and Sutherland, and had observed the way of life of the tinkers there before coming to Shetland. I admired their enterprise in setting out with their own wagon in this fashion, and more particularly I admire the spirit of a woman who can do this whilst bearing a family.

The caravan was eventually brought across the Sound in an old wartime landing craft which the islanders used for shifting cattle, tractors and other heavy items. This extraordinary, cumbersome and leaky craft was at that time their only means of moving anything which was too big for the mailboat. It had been acquired in the early 1960s; before that the islanders had had a recurring problem with moving cattle off the island when they were sold at the end of the summer. The last straw was when the County Council provided a boat to uplift and ship the cattle to Voe, a matter of five miles, and the crofters received bills for £12 per head for moving the cattle. This was at a time when a good price for a cow was £20, so the islanders were horrified and severely out of pocket. Something had to be done about the transport problem, so with some help from the Crofters Commission and a good deal of fund-raising amongst the islanders themselves, the barge was located in Orkney and shipped to Papa on the Northern Lighthouse Board supply boat. The barge was unloaded in House Voe and stands on the beach there still. (Ironically enough, when the islanders offered to pay the Lighthouse Board men for their help, they would accept no payment.) She was used every summer for many years, towed to Sandness and back by the mailboat, and getting her in and out of the water required every ounce of available manpower on the island. Wooden, heavy, about thirty feet long and shaped like an outsize coffin, the barge is a monument to the import and export problems of life on a small island.

When we took over the caravan, we moved it to a spot beside the end of an old byre to give us shelter. On the other three sides old stone walls prevented the wind from getting underneath the van. She stood very snugly in this tiny enclosure, and although she rocked a bit in a gale she could never have really moved. She was heavily built of thick wood, not in the least like the modern work-men's hut of unsubstantial tin and fibreglass.

Gavin had installed a miniature solid fuel range in the caravan complete with stove pipe, and this was a delight to me. I have learned a lot since then about the idiosyncrasies of solid fuel cookers and how to cook on them; their moods are entirely governed by the wind, and whilst you may have a roaring fire one day and an oven that is perfect for baking, another day you will get a sluggish fire and no heat at all for your oven. I made bread regularly in this little stove; it had a tiny oven in which two loaf tins just fitted.

Although I now live in a fairly big house, the miniature dwelling in which we started our life on Papa Stour was a good beginning. Whilst not proof against the icy fingers of a northerly gale, the cara-van was snug and made a cosy little home for the two of us through that first winter.

But we knew this could not be permanent. We liked living on Papa Stour and had agreed to join in the fishing boat project, but we would simply have to have better accommodation. The island was dotted with derelict houses, and there were several empty ones that were not derelict at all. We approached everyone we could think of, but the response was invariably negative. Reasons varied but seemed very unconvincing. I can understand it a lot better now than I did then. As far as the local folk were concerned we might just as well have come from another planet, we were so different from them, and they just could not believe that this was what we really wanted.

We did at one point obtain permission from the local Education Committee to live in the school house, which was unoccupied since the school was closed. This was to be on a caretaker basis— we paid no rent, but we agreed to look after the place and meet any expenses in that respect, and we could be asked to leave at two weeks' notice at any time. Obviously we could not make a home there on those terms; anyway, the house was badly laid out and the garden was on the poorest soil on the island.

In the course of our correspondence with the local education authorities we were asked how we proposed to make a living on Papa Stour. At the time I thought this was extremely impertinent; our financial affairs were no concern of theirs, particularly as they did not want any rent. I still find their query unjustifiable, but admit that knowing what I know now, this is invariably the unspoken question in my mind when I meet someone who expresses a wish to live on Papa Stour. At times people have lived here with the help of social security benefits, but after a time the authorities have applied pressure to ensure that one of the household finds a job on the mainland. Often then the wife can't cope: life can become very tedious and difficult with young children and the man away. Small things like a shortage of paraffin or a tilley lamp that won't light take on a great importance on a dark November night with the prospect of weeks with nothing but candles from four o'clock to bedtime. He might fail to send any money home or start seeking other female company on the mainland.

We have had family break-ups. We had one episode where practically everyone on the island was supplying fuel to a family whilst the man was away supposedly working. People here are wonderfully supportive to a family if one of the parents is away for any reason, and I know if I am here on my own with the children I have only to ask if I need help should the generator refuse to start, of if I need to shift a barrel of fuel.

I have learned a lot about giving and receiving help. Often it's just a matter of someone coming in for a few minutes' chat. When the oldest person you've spoken to all day is a six-year-old, however articulate and original she may be you feel very glad for a few minutes of adult company.

Of all the empty houses on the island, the one I best liked the look of was the manse. We approached the Church of Scotland in Edinburgh, and at first it seemed as if they didn't know they had a manse on Papa Stour. It was many years since the island had had a resident minister. In the 1960s the teacher's husband was the lay missionary here but they had lived at the schoolhouse. The manse had been occupied on and off by caretaker tenants, but was in a state of considerable neglect. It was a large house as they go on Papa Stour; although two up and two down, the roof had been raised to give good-sized bedrooms upstairs, and it had dormer windows which are a traditional and attractive feature of many Shetland houses. In addition there was a single-story building of two rooms attached to the south end of the house. Originally this was the mission hall and served as the school before the present school was built. Our oldest inhabitant can remember coming to school here in the late 1890s. This part never had a ceiling put in, the roof is neatly lined with wood and retains a rather church-like appearance. Other attractions were that the house had a bathroom with a flush toilet, a septic tank, and hot and cold running water from a Truburn stove—things which none of the other empty houses had with the exception of the school. Unfortunately, the bathroom was housed in an unsightly flat-roof box attached to the front of the house and it detracted considerably from the appearance of the house; it must have been added before planning permission became compulsory, as I can't imagine such an eyesore being acceptable to our environment-conscious planners today.

The reaction of the Church was to stall. Their eventual excuse was that there was some talk of a resident nurse being installed on the island, and if this came about she was to live in the manse. This seemed unlikely to us, so undeterred off we went to the Nursing Officer in Lerwick, who assured us that they had no intention of putting a nurse on Papa Stour. The manse was a nice house and we set our beam on it. They had put us off, but they had not heard the last of us.

Christmas and New Year came and went and we continued to walk about amongst the ruined crofthouses speculating as to whether we could ever acquire one and rebuild it. Where crofters had left the island in search of a better life their land had been amalgamated into neighbouring crofts and their houses had been allowed to fall into decay, or used as hay byres or shelter for lambs. Local crofters were not keen to have incomers setting up house in amongst their sheep; and like farmers everywhere they certainly did not want to give up any land.

By this time some friends had taken over one of the dispossessed crofts called East Toon, and had moved into a house there. There were two other ruins on their croft and they said we could have whichever we wanted together with the yard or garden that went with it. Their croft was not sufficiently established for them to worry about our disturbing their stock, and their whole attitude was different from that of the islanders. Mariane and Darryl had arrived on the island a few months before us and were in much the same position as ourselves, except that they had a better idea than we had about what they wanted to do. It had been their ambition for some years to try their hand at farming. Both the ruins on the East Toon croft were down to just a few feet of wall and a couple of gables, so if we were to rebuild one of these we would need some temporary accommodation while we did it.

In the spring I knew that our longed-for baby was on the way. This seemed a good time to do something we had talked about for years, but had never managed to get around to. Kevin and I went to Lerwick and got married. I did not want any celebrations or receptions, but it seemed that we could not escape them. Other people made them happen. We had a party in Lerwick; another on the boat returning to the isle—it was a blustery March day and I felt glad of the warmth of that celebratory spirit—and yet another in the island schoolroom. Almost everyone came to it, and it is still remembered with enthusiasm. With the ageing and diminishing population, together with the coming of television, community life on the island was at a virtual standstill before the arrival of the newcomers. The schoolroom doubles as a community hall, and I think this must have been the first party there for years. The islanders, whom we didn't know very well then, seemed delighted at the prospect of a party; they lent glasses and brought jugs of milk and insisted on doing all the clearing up afterwards, even to scrubbing the floor. I recall two elderly men greeting each other there and it was obvious that they had not spoken to each other for years although they lived only a few minutes' walk away.

We danced eightsome reels to a battery-operated record player, and we even had a surprise three-tier wedding cake, baked by our friends in three separate houses the previous night and put together in a most unique way. This was before any of us had mastered our solid fuel stoves, and baking a cake was an intrepid undertaking the result of which could not be foretold. However, the enthusiasm and good vibrations that went into that cake far outweighed the lack of culinary expertise.

My mother wrote from England that she was pleased that we were getting married at last. She is the traditional sort and would have liked to make us a wedding present of the family silver or a set of monogrammed bed linen, but she realised that would hardly be suitable in our present circumstances, so what could she give us? I sent back a prompt reply: please could we have a wooden sectional hut which we could erect next to our ruin on Papa Stour? Just how my parents reacted to this request I shall never know. However, they did not fail me, and within a few weeks the sections started to arrive. Some came on the mail boat, some were towed across the Sound behind it and poled ashore onto the island, others were floated across the Voe in a suitable wind to the beach nearest to our home. Many helpful hands made light work of erecting our new dwelling, and to keep it from blowing away Kevin devised an ingenious scheme with heavy gauge wire running through pipes attached to the ridge beams and secured outside to stakes set in concrete. This was an essential precaution and worked very well; the hut never did blow away or sustain any damage (though it was the weather that eventually proved our undoing). We named it Far East and lived there for just over a year, but the winter weather caused us a good deal of concern once we had the baby. It was like being in a matchbox in a hurricane. The walls bulged inward with the weight of the wind on them, and if someone was mad enough to open the door our eyes immediately went to the roof in expectation that it might take off. One night shortly after New Year stands out horribly clearly to this day. It is the custom over the New Year period to make a round of all the houses drinking a goodwill dram at each. On this particular windy night three of the island men called in at Far East on their tour of the eastern peninsula; they had already been to several houses and arrived in fine fettle. We let them in quickly, closed the door on the wind and settled down to the business of wishing each other a good new year.

We had no dram glasses, but found that limpet shells served very well; we had some very big ones as we were in the habit of gathering limpets occasionally as a treat for the cat. In due course our visitors decided to continue on their journey, but because we were all feeling so mellow their departure took rather a long time. Kevin was standing by the door at the ready but every time they made to move out one would crack another joke or someone started looking for his hat, his muffler or his bottle. I don't think they ever realised the state of panic we were in as they eventually found their way out into the weather shouting cheerful expressions of goodwill as they went.

The hut was three times the size of the caravan and it felt like a palace. The other newcomers came up with a most inspired wedding gift in the shape of an old stove called a Modern Mistress—a beautiful stove with a steel top which gets hot all over; they look lovely if kept shiny with steel wool or emery paper. It took a lot of cleaning, however, and gobbled up coal at a most alarming rate. It kept us warm and we did all the cooking on it, and could always have a large pan of hot water at the ready even if it was cooking at the same time. The water had to be carried from East Toon and we never got as far as laying it on to the hut. Kevin built a platform for the bed, and we had shelves, worktops and a sink; the only furniture we had was a Greenland chest and an antique treadle sewing machine, although while I was away having the baby Kevin built a remarkable armchair out of a fishbox and some driftwood; it is still our only armchair, and greatly prized.

We planted the garden with vegetables and thought a lot about rebuilding the ruined house at Far East; it was a lovely spot and felt very good. We could see both the Papa pier and the Sandness pier, which was useful, since watching out for boats had become part of our way of life.

Our baby girl arrived in October, and the responsibility of it began to dawn on us. On three separate nights during that winter I took the baby and stayed the night at East Toon because of the way the hut was shuddering and shaking in the wind. It was one thing for Kevin and I to live like this if we chose, but we certainly could not expose our precious and helpless infant to such dangers. We agreed that we could not spend another winter in the hut, but we had as yet no definite plans for the ruin.

The empty manse was still in the back of our minds. It was a fine house and it was deteriorating simply as a result of neglect. I sent another barrage of letters to the church authorities in Edinburgh, and then Kevin started to telephone them. Once a week without fail he would make a collection of tenpenny pieces, go off to the callbox beside the post office and telephone through to Edinburgh to remind them about their manse on Papa Stour. Eventually they said he should go down to Edinburgh and talk about it, so he was on the next boat south. Once there, all the problems seemed to dissolve, and he came back triumphant. At long last we were to have a real roof over our heads. It was to be on a caretaker basis with three months' notice, but it was a real house and we felt very relieved at this in spite of the lack of security that went with it. In fact, as long as we behaved ourselves we could foresee no reason for their ever wanting to evict us.

Four years later the Church of Scotland Home Board agreed to sell the manse to us along with its outbuildings and two yards; the only provisions were that it should no longer be called the manse and that we should not sell liquor. The latter has not been difficult to comply with, but everyone except us still calls it the manse.

Now that the house belongs to us we have really begun to put down roots. We have undertaken extensive renovation and improvements since the house became our own, even though many would question the advisability of investing money in a property on an island where living is so precarious. To me the idea of the depopulation of Papa Stour is abhorrent, but not unthinkable. It nearly happened just before we got here.

With the population standing at sixteen, the school closed and no children living on the isle, the prospect for its continuing to be an inhabited island did indeed look bleak. Some of the islanders were in the process of making plans to move away; others had already bought houses on the mainland. The arrival of ourselves and others like us stemmed the tide, but as the years have gone by things have become more difficult for all of us. Farming and crofting have run into enormous problems, partly as a result of membership in the European Common Market (which Orkney and Shetland voted against joining); partly due to several seasons of bad weather; inflation has hit us all, and for everyone the cost of living is rising at a higher rate than earnings. But it seems worthwhile to me, and I believe in the continued existence of Papa Stour. Just how the island can be made viable in the 1980s isn't at all clear. Although there is a certain amount of apathy in some departments of the civil service, there are undoubtedly many in the Shetland Islands Council who would view the total depopulation of Papa Stour with very great sadness; and it would be very bad publicity for Shetland. I can just see the banner headlines: "Another St. Kilda" with a picture of a crofter leading the last cow down to the waiting boat. I know that if someone came up with a good project that could provide employment for just a few people, money could be made available by the local authority and the Highland Board to get such a project under way. All we need is the good idea.

Chapter 4
Babies come along

Human biology, and certainly the reproductive aspects, was skated over in my education, but now I would like to know a great deal more about how the body works. In my dealings with the medical profession I find that much is shrouded in mystique, and that doctors are not being open with us. When I put this to a general practitioner recently, he replied that most of his patients didn't want to know; they just wanted to do what the doctor advised. If this is true, it is a symptom of a very unsatisfactory state of mind. Our bodies are first and foremost our own responsibility.

In her first pregnancy a woman does not know what is happening to her, but I would suggest that listening to the voice within and feeling the feelings within will give a mother more peace of mind than any number of visits to the clinic. Pregnancy should be a time of peace and tranquility, when the mother puts her best efforts into nurturing the growing life within her and avoids distractions; we have been conditioned to think that we need doctors and nurses far more than we actually do.

Unless specifically called over, the doctor visits Papa Stour twice a year. There is no nurse on the isle, but the District Nurse from the mainland visits occasionally. The nursing profession is very strict about keeping the rules it has made for itself. A pregnant woman is supposed to be seen by a midwife every month until the last eight weeks, and after that she should be checked every week until her baby is born.

It is very difficult for the doctor or nurse to get to Papa Stour; it means taking at least half a day away from routine work and also that they are not available for emergency duties. When they get here they probably have to walk several miles between the different houses, all of which is time-consuming and tiring for a busy person not used to long walks. Sometimes several of us have gathered at one house if we wanted to see the doctor, but that is no good when one is pregnant as he is unlikely to get a realistic blood pressure reading from a woman who has just done a lengthy and energetic walk.

A home birth in Shetland is a rare event. Most doctors feel far happier with their patients in hospital in Lerwick, as this is where all the equipment is should any emergency arise. With our first baby I was advised that in view of my age I should go to the town two weeks before the baby was due in case of a bad spell of weather which might cut the island off.

It turned out that I did have a slight complication when seven months pregnant, and I awoke one morning exhibiting signs of a miscarriage. I went to bed and Kevin went to telephone the doctor. As luck would have it it happened to be the day the District Nurse came in to do one of her periodic check-ups, so she came to see me and announced that I should go straight to hospital. I felt as fit as a flea, and knowing what I now know I should have stayed a couple of days in bed and told no-one of my symptoms. Hospital consisted of a week in bed on barbiturates. I could hardly have been more miserable.

Getting to hospital was hazardous. I should have been carried down to the pier on a stretcher, but nobody thought of it at the time and not many people were about. It was a sweltering day in August, and I had the option of a mile's walk over rough ground with several fences to climb or a bumpy ride on the back of a tractor.

I chose the latter—standing balanced with my legs bent so as not to jar my bulging tummy. It was the day of the local agricultural show on the mainland and the boat was crowded with people going for a merry day out. I sat on a fishbox and didn't know whether I was coming or going. The nurse was nervous and kept asking if I was haemorrhaging; fortunately I wasn't and I didn't, but I would have done better to have stayed at home.

After a couple of weeks in hospital it was clear that the miscarriage had been averted, and with some reluctance they allowed me to return to the island. I went back to Lerwick two weeks before the baby was due and stayed with friends until the birth.

Our daughter was the most beautiful and perfect little thing I had ever seen, and she was almost a model baby. I had a little trouble learning to breastfeed her, mainly due to my own lack of confidence and to the fact that she was always sound asleep at the official feeding times laid down by the hospital, but after the first few days we never looked back. I have never liked the idea of feeding babies with bottles—plastic teats seem slightly obscene somehow—but I have spoken to women who obviously feel the opposite. One said "I couldn't breastfeed, it would make me feel like a cow." The hospital staff was concerned that I should take a bottle home with me with a supply of powdered milk, and that I should know all about the sterilising routine. I was determined not to have my confidence undermined, and although I kept these artificial aids by me I never had need of them. Getting supplies from the mainland takes time, especially in winter, and for this reason alone I would not have wanted to rely on powdered milk which only has a limited life in the packet.

Given a quiet life and a minimum of distractions most women can breastfeed their babies, and I think that if she is physically able a mother owes it to her child to feed it for at least the first nine months. If she is not prepared to devote this time to it she does not deserve to have a baby. Since the baby is attached within the mother for nine months I have come to the conclusion that the ideal length of time for it to be attached on the outside is also nine months: a shorter time and you are weaning it too soon, a longer time and the baby gets too clever and knowing and determines never to give up.

When it was time to feed my baby on solids I bought baby cereals and made up feeds myself with the fruit and vegetables I had; later she had just what we had mashed up. None of our three children has ever had a taste of a tin or jar of manufactured food. I was once told that a well-known brand of tinned baby food contained extra sugar designed to make it taste attractive to the mother. Babies can eat much blander food than adults and I consider such a sales gimmick to be quite immoral.

Kevin had been an only child, and regretted not having had any brothers or sisters. The very day after our little girl was born he was talking about our having another baby. I was feeling a bit tired at the time but agreed that it would probably happen sooner or later, and exactly two years later we had a little boy, Alan. That was lovely, just what we wanted. What I had not bargained for was number three. I knew after Alan was born that I should go to the mainland and get some family planning advice, but I kept putting it off as it was such an upheaval; it would have meant leaving our daughter, but I would have had to take the baby as I was feeding him. We all had a bad attack of flu and I felt jaded and lethargic. It was winter, which meant I would certainly have to spend a night on the mainland, but it could easily turn into a week if the weather was bad. We have many marvellously hospitable and understanding friends on the mainland, but to descend on them with a young baby, nappies and all, for an indefinite period seemed rather an imposition, so I just didn't go.

The result was that six months after our second baby was born I started to have that queasy feeling all over again. I felt very alarmed indeed. I was tired; our boy did not sleep as well as the little girl and seemed a lot more demanding. I seriously doubted whether I could cope. Obviously I would just have to. We tried to practise positive thinking, and consoled ourselves with the thought that this was meant to be and all would be for the best. And as the pregnancy went on I did grow stronger and stronger, and began to feel happier about it. I enjoyed being pregnant, and once I weaned Alan, whom I was still feeding at the time of conception, I was able to concentrate my strength more on the new baby. Now, of course, Iain is as dear to us as any of them, and we are very glad that we have three children. It is clear to me now how in days gone by women became completely worn out by childbirth at quite an early age. Without contraceptives most women could probably have a baby every year or so; even given the family back-up which was more prevalent then than it is today this would put an enormous drain on a woman's energy, and certainly would allow her no time at all to think of herself and whether she had any purpose in this world other than being a mother.

There is sixteen months between our two little boys, and it was a full two years after our youngest was born that I began to feel strong again. You do not realise that you are weak; you just struggle on. But when the realisation came one spring morning that I actually felt like bouncing about with energy it was a very pleasant shock. I made sure that I saw to the family planning in good time after number three.

All our babies were born in the same bed in the same delivery room in the same hospital. There is a small maternity hospital of eleven beds in Lerwick, and any complicated cases are flown to

Aberdeen. Fortunately I was never one of these, but going off to Lerwick for a spell was always an upheaval, especially as our family grew. They like you to stay on the mainland for ten days after the birth so that the midwife can check you every day, but I was always longing to get back so that we could all be together in our own home. I did seriously consider having our second baby at home; our doctor understood how we felt and would not have refused to attend me, and I felt confident that nothing would go wrong. However, I could never have forgiven myself if for instance the baby had needed a blood transfusion or oxygen and the dash to hospital had taken too long, added to which was the thought of an ambulance flight whilst in labour. I would hate to be the object of such an emergency. So I took the safe way and went to hospital in plenty of time.

Thor, a boy who is just a few days older than our daughter, was born on the island. His mother is strong in body and spirit and this was her third baby, but the great thing was that she had complete faith that all would be well, and indeed it was.

Returning to the island with a new baby was always a moving experience for us, and I suspect it was for the boatmen too—could they ever carry a more precious cargo? Until the arrival of the newcomers babies had stopped arriving as far as the islanders were concerned, though since then one young Shetland couple has returned to the isle to live and has had another baby. Taking the week-old baby from the hospital where it had been maintained in a temperature of $75°$ F, and putting it in an open boat in bad weather, always gave me a bit of a fright, but they all seemed very hardy and appeared not to notice. Only Iain, who was dumped on the rocks at Hamna Voe in his carry-cot, gave a whimper of protest as if to say that this was hardly the place for him at this age. It was February and we had waited several days to get home; on the day they came out for us a bad north wind got up and the *Venture* had to run back into Hamna Voe on the south side of the isle; there is no pier there but at high water you can nose a boat in and go ashore on the rocks.

I try to get the children out of doors whenever I can, as it seems to relieve a lot of their tensions if they can just be out in the fresh air for even a few minutes. They will come in again and settle down for a new game, when before they went out they seemed to be feeling just bored and destructive. No traffic passes our house except for an occasional tractor, and I know that we are very privileged to have this freedom for our children.

Whilst we do not have the variety of wildlife that is to be seen in the English countryside, the children are learning to recognise the birds and sea creatures that are here. In spring we hear the eider ducks making seductive noises to their mates down at the beach, and later on we see the mother with five or six little ones swimming behind. We also see that within a couple of weeks the families are reduced to one or two as the black-backed gulls prey upon them.

The facts of life can be explained easily and naturally in the country, where birth and death are such frequent occurences, yet confusion can still arise, as I found when speaking to four-year-old Alan about a new-born lamb we had seen. I told him how it had been born and then, quite naturally I thought, went on to say how I had had three babies born in much the same way. He thought about it quietly for a few moments and then said "Yes mum, but did you ever have a lamb?"

It seems essential to me that my children grow up close to nature with all its beauty and all its cruelty. I sometimes find myself wanting to prevent them from seeing the nasty things—a dead lamb with its eyes pecked out—but really it is better if they know that these things happen. A bigger problem which they will one day have to see is the cruelty of humankind. I grew up in very sheltered surroundings myself, and I feel it would be better if they had a clearer idea than I did of what the world is really like.

Chapter 5
The economic problem

Papa Stour has always been a fishing and farming community, but in days gone by the men had to go away to find employment, sending money home to supplement the family income. There are men here now who spent many years at the whaling in South Georgia; others have travelled the world with the merchant navy. Shetlanders are born seamen, and a shipping company would often take on a Shetlander in preference to another man, as he could be relied upon to keep a cool head at sea.

The land was worked by older men, women and children. They provided a great deal of their own food, kept a pig, used skins of their own animals for footwear and many household objects, and were very self-sufficient. There was much hardship; landlords were often inhumane, and would put a family out of their house if they could not pay the rent. The men who were at home were contracted to fish for the landlord and to sell their catch to him at the price specified by him. The haaf fishing, as it was called, was hard and dangerous work and lives were not infrequently lost.

To be fair, it seems that the landlords themselves were hardpressed to maintain their standard of living and provide what their masters demanded of them, so they felt compelled to extract as much as they possibly could from the peasants. There is no doubt that the ordinary people of Shetland have a history of being very down-trodden. Everyone lived in fear of the factor, and he lived in fear of the laird.

The establishment of the Crofters' Commission and the investigations of the Truck Commission at the end of the last century did much to improve the lot of the poorer people, and since then the welfare state has been established and there is more security for all.

There are only two people on Papa Stour in full-time employment—the teacher and the postmistress. There are one or two other part-time jobs, and the boatmen are paid to bring the mails from Sandness three times a week, but the chief source of income is crofting. Since the second world war self-sufficiency has gone by the board in favour of intensive sheep farming, and the islanders themselves admit that it is the ruination of the land.

Before the war sheep were restricted to the common grazings or scattald on the west side of the isle, and the land to the east, which is by Shetland standards good arable, was reserved for cattle and growing crops. Agricultural machinery did not arrive much before the 1950s and is still very limited. Before that the land was dug with the Shetland spade, the diggers working side by side in teams of three or more. The steady decline in population has meant that less and less land could be cultivated and fewer and fewer cattle could be kept, and now each croft has a small amount of cultivated land on which they grow potatoes, oats if they have a cow, and turnips for winter feed. They also reserve a field for hay, and kale is grown for the sheep in a walled yard. The rest of the land is under grass and fully stocked with sheep, but everywhere there are the signs of the boundaries of the old rigs, and all this land was once cultivated. In some places it is so overgrazed that the combination of sheep, wind and weather is turning the land into sand dunes. The grass struggles through the sand only to be immediately cropped by the sheep, then a wind blows sand up from the beach and covers what green there is.

Yet the sheep appear to be the only way that people can continue to make a livelihood here. With the shortage of capital, machinery and manpower, this has become the only alternative left to them. The weather can make the harvesting of corn very uncertain—it is not unusual for them to bring it home in late October—and haymaking is a prolonged and often disastrous affair, with persistent rain leaching the goodness out of the cut grass and preventing the crofter from getting it dried.

Wool is rooed in June and July; Shetland sheep have a different sort of fleece from other sheep, and it is pulled out rather than sheared. The wool is sold locally, and the price is extraordinarily low when one compares it with the price of a ball of wool in a shop.

Lambs are sold at the end of the summer, and a number of breeding ewes are kept on the croft to produce next spring's crop of lambs. The problems of selling stock from a small island are depressing: a buyer comes to the island in September, but as there is usually only one who is prepared to come, one must accept his price or not sell. Then the sheep have to be shipped out from the island at considerable expense. The alternative is to send them to the market on the mainland, but they too have to be shipped, possibly spend a night or two in a borrowed field, and then transported by road; if the weather is bad one might miss the market altogether. There is no easy solution to this problem; transport is becoming more and more expensive, and it is very difficult to organise from the island.

Crofters also make money from cattle; whether if they costed out the hours of work put into raising them and growing feed for them they would make a clear profit is quite another matter, but in a good year an eighteen-month-old bullock or heifer will fetch several hundred pounds. Again there is the problem of selling to the solitary buyer who visits the island; sometimes two buyers come together, but they will agree between them in advance as to the top price to be paid. Cows provide milk for one or more households, but in some cases the greater part of the milk is fed back to the calves. Dairy work is time consuming and exacting, and with the labour shortage which exists not many people find the time to make butter or cheese.

It is obvious that the land is not in good heart and that continuous grazing by sheep is not going to improve matters. Papa Stour used to be known for the scent of its wild flowers—we are told that the fishermen could smell them out at sea—but now the grass is cropped very short by the sheep and the flowers, although they do exist, are microscopic. I once asked a visiting professor of botany what it would be like here were it not for the sheep; his eyes lit up and he went into ecstasies of enthusiasm about the many and varied species of flora which are confined to this part of the world and more particularly to this island, and about the variety and height of the vegetation which would grow here.

We came with no idea of how we could make a living here, but when we had the opportunity to take a share in the shell-fishing boat we thought we had solved that particular problem.

Unfortunately we hadn't. In due course the *Quest* arrived at the isle. She was built in Orkney, and Kevin and Gavin went down to

Burray to watch her trials and bring her back to Papa Stour. It all took longer than we expected; they had to wait for several foggy days on the mainland for a flight to Orkney, and coming back they had to put into Scalloway for some modifications to the winch. We were living in the hut at Far East and had no telephone there; I must have spent three solid days staring at the horizon at the south end of the Sound in my eagerness to make the first sighting of the new boat. She impressed me with her strength and solidity and also with her equipment—echosounder, VHF radio, sink, and gas cooker. There were two bunks for'ard—everything was bright and new, and they were ready to start work. We found out later that she was so solidly built (larch on oak) that she was altogether too heavy for the thirty horsepower engine with which she was fitted, and that the square stern was quite a hazard. Although this had the advantage of providing extra room on board it did make her difficult to handle, especially since she was underpowered. You have to come away from both the Sandness pier and the Papa pier in reverse, and the transom stern provided considerable resistance and made things dangerous in an onshore wind.

The skipper who trained them was a fisherman who had first gone to sea in the days when the Shetland fleet was still under sail; he is a hard and efficient man who soon taught Gavin and Kevin what they had to do, and saw to it that they went out in all weathers and learned to handle their boat and work their creels in the rough seas and difficult tides that meet around Papa Stour. They had spent the previous months making two hundred creels; coils and coils of rope were bought and the creels were assembled into leaders of twenty creels each. As well as crabs and lobsters, a variety of other rarely seen sea creatures are caught in the creels—starfish, sea urchins, little green crabs, dogfish, wrass, octopus and conger eels. After they have been lifted the creels are re-baited and shot overboard again, in the same place if it has proved productive or in a different spot if a change in the weather indicates that this one would not be safe. Running repairs have to be carried out on the creels whilst they are on board as they can become damaged if they bump against rocks in a swell, so a netting needle and twine, hammer and nails are carried on board the boat. Fishing at any period of the year is uncertain, and it is not uncommon to lose whole leaders of creels if the weather turns bad and the boat cannot get out to rescue them. The wind can blow them ashore and rough seas will break them up on the rocks.

Kevin and Gavin worked but the crabs just were not there. One can always catch crabs, but to catch them in the quantities which they needed to in order to pay off the boat and provide for two families was another matter. There was only one buyer of crabs in Shetland and the price was miserable. The fisherman who takes all the risks makes far less than the middle man, the fishmongers and the restaurant owners.

From what I have seen of the fishing industry I would say that any fish that you see on the fishmonger's slab is worth its weight in gold. Over the years I must have spent hours and hours scanning the sea trying to pick out our small boat, observing the state of the tide, feeling the wind picking up, listening to the shipping forecast. It is a very dangerous occupation, and every year the sea takes its toll of fishermen's lives.

The fishing was certainly poor—crabs were scarce, lobsters scarcer. Long lining was tried, but only briefly. A long line requires a good deal of preparation as it is sixty fathoms long and has sixty baited hooks; baited with piltocks in our case, though in the old days shellfish were often used, the women and children spending long hours gathering the limpets or mussels and then baiting the lines. The line is set on the edge of a fast tide and hauled up four hours later. They had hopes of catching halibut, which were once plentiful around here and which fetch a good price, but were not successful. They caught some good fish, including dogfish and a two-hundred pound skate, but found them impossible to sell in the local market.

Some of the larger Shetland fishing boats make regular runs to Aberdeen to land their catch, and no doubt better prices can usually be obtained there than in the local markets. The fact that the price of crabs was so low and that some good fish were un-saleable was certainly discouraging. We could catch any amount of mackerel at the time we had the *Quest*, but no one would buy them except at a very low price for fish meal. Now there is a good local market for mackerel, and many boats with sophisticated gear come around Papa Stour in the summer.

At the end of the first season our partner decided to leave, and this left the Highland Board with the problem of whether to take the *Quest* away and sell it, or hand it over to Kevin. In spite of his brief experience they decided on the latter course.

So Kevin became the skipper of the *Quest*, and took on a new partner. One of the first things that happened was that we had a phone call early one autumn morning from the post office to tell us that she was dragging her moorings in Housa Voe. The wind was blowing strongly from the west, and whilst she wasn't in any immediate danger, she obviously wasn't safely moored. Through the worst part of the winter we rarely leave boats in Housa Voe as it is dangerously exposed to wind and sea; the safest moorings are in Culla Voe, which is L-shaped and comparatively sheltered on all sides. Kevin went down to the pier and rowed off to the boat; going off in an eight-foot fibreglass pram dinghy is not the sort of thing that anyone does in a force nine gale if they can possibly avoid it, but the boat was extremely important to us and Kevin is able to keep a cool head in such situations. As a precaution he took a line with him which was made fast at the pier, and Dave his crewman stood by ready to haul him in should the dinghy capsize. He got aboard the *Quest* successfully, brought her up ahead of her original moorings and put out an additional anchor, after which she held without giving any further cause for concern.

They got very little fishing through the winter as the weather was too stormy, but Kevin made another hundred creels for the coming season. In March they set to with a will, but the bad weather continued and they lost several leaders of creels. Crabs seemed just as scarce, and we were barely managing to pay the fuel costs on the boat. Lack of experience undoubtedly had a lot to do with it; if you own the boat, weathering a bad season or two may well be possible, but in our case we had the burden of a loan, and were not only expected to make substantial repayments every quarter, but pay the interest on the loan too. The Board fully understood the situation, and accepted that we were unable to pay, but after some months of struggling like this they took action and Kevin was advised that he should sell the boat. The day I watched her steaming through the Sound for the last time was a sad one indeed.

The *Quest* was bought by a man in the south mainland of Shetland, and her history since leaving Papa Stour has not been without distinction. There was a bad air crash at Sumburgh in the autumn of 1979 when a plane ran off the runway and went into the sea. The *Quest* was the first boat on the scene and picked up seven of the survivors.

Although we constantly criticise the local authority for neglecting rural areas, and especially the small islands, it must be said that when newcomers first came to Papa Stour efforts were undoubtedly made to revitalise the island. The provision of the *Quest* was intended to make a living for two families and to create better communications with the mainland. As well as this, an opportunity was provided for inhabitants of the island to enter the Shetland knitting industry. The idea required a bit of adjustment for most of us. In England men just don't knit; in Shetland, however, before the coming of the oil industry, knitting was a common form of employment amongst men and women alike. There were knitting factories in many of the remoter areas, and it was very common to find knitting machines in houses both in the rural areas and in the town. It was and still is a cottage industry, though many have now forsaken their machines for higher paid work with the oil.

A co-operative knitwear firm based in Lerwick decided to send four industrial knitting machines and an instructor to Papa Stour for a period of three months to enable some of the newcomers to learn to knit. This was while we were waiting for the *Quest* to be built, so Kevin and I both took the opportunity to learn. The idea was that those who learned should knit for this firm full-time once the course was over. We pointed out that some of us would not be able to do this because we were already committed to the fishing boat. In fact at this time no one really wanted to commit themselves to knitting, and no secret was made of this. Nevertheless, they would teach us, and they would pay us while we were learning. Kevin earned £16 a week while I earned £12.50 for identical work. I can hardly believe this now in these days of equal pay, and I did remonstrate with our instructor, but of course it was quite out of his hands, and I could hardly make a big issue of it without upsetting the prospects for everyone else.

We are very glad now that we had the opportunity to learn to knit. The firm went into liquidation a few months after we had completed our course, but by that time Kevin was making creels ready for the arrival of the boat, and I was expecting a baby. After the *Quest* was sold we bought a second-hand industrial knitting machine, and this has become a standby as a source of income. We usually knit for a Lerwick firm—they supply the wool and we knit up jumpers and send them out for finishing and dressing. It is rather tedious and repetitive work, but the important thing is that Kevin can earn money without leaving the island.

Another possibility as income is tourists. As we are isolated and living in such a small community I am aware that we lack the stimulation of meeting new people regularly, and also that the children meet so few others of their own age. To this end, and also with the hopes of financial gain, we bought three small caravans to let to summer visitors.

We arranged to buy the caravans before we had any idea of how we could get them onto the island. Certainly they were quite beyond the capabilities of the mailboat, which is only twenty-five feet long. I did feel confident that somehow a way would be found to get them onto Papa Stour. I thought of approaching one of the oil companies who have been known to provide a helicopter to assist in such matters for the publicity value, but I came to the conclusion that for such a company to help it would need to be for the communal good rather than for my personal benefit. We enquired about hiring a boat to bring them, but the cost would have been prohibitive. This led us to ask ourselves whether it was right that we should be at such a disadvantage in regard to communications with the mainland. Although in the short term it was my caravans which I was concerned about, it did strike me that we on Papa Stour were severely disadvantaged if the largest boat we could call on for transport was a privately owned twenty-five foot open boat. Ferries do come quite high on the Shetland Islands Council rates schedule, and whilst the larger islands now have a roll-on roll-off service several times a day we have nothing of the sort. Of course such a service would not be feasible here with the winter seas we get in the Sound of Papa, but undoubtedly there was room for improvement. In conjunction with the neighbouring island of Foula, which is far more isolated than we are, we launched a petition asking the local authority to provide us with a boat service for heavy goods such as caravans, vehicles and fuel. It was signed by every adult who was a resident on Foula and Papa Stour at the time; fortunately it fell on sympathetic ears and we didn't have the fight we anticipated over this. It was arranged that the *Spes Clara*, an elderly eighty-foot ex-fishing boat which is on permanent charter to the Shetland Islands Council, should visit our two islands up to four times a year.

The service the county has provided leaves a good deal to be desired, but at least coal no longer has to be uplifted bag by bag from Sandness. Every household here takes in an average of three tons of coal a year, as there is no peat on the island. When sold at the end of summer, lambs no longer have to be shipped out a few at a time in the *Venture*; this used to entail many runs to Sandness and countless sluicings-down of the mailboat afterwards to remove their excrement. The total number of lambs sold runs into hundreds, and now these all leave on the one day in the hold of the *Spes Clara*. Formerly each lamb had to be individually manhandled on the pier at Sandness as there are no fences or temporary hurdles available there, but now they are unloaded into pens on the dock at Lerwick, and from the island crofter's point of view the operation of disposing of the lambs is simplified considerably. Cattle which used to go out with the barge are now also shipped out on the *Spes Clara*, and whilst no one is happy to see a cow which they have nurtured from the day it was born hoisted aboard the boat in a sling, hearts have to be hardened to such things.

Building materials such as cement and timber are delivered direct from Lerwick on the *Spes Clara* where hitherto each person who had goods ordered had them sent by lorry to Sandness and then brought them across in the *Venture* bit by bit.

Problems arise because the *Spes Clara* is committed to doing two runs a week from Lerwick to Out Skerries, a group of islands on the east side of Shetland; she is the mailboat for Skerries as well as their supply boat and they only get mail there twice a week. This means that she can only come to Papa and Foula at the weekends, and she has been known to arrive here at seven o'clock on a Sunday morning to unload twenty tons of coal. I don't know if it comes as a surprise to those who organise these things to know that Papa folk enjoy a day off work as much as anyone else. The *Spes Clara* men of course get good overtime rates for this work, but the islanders get an extra hard day's unpaid work in between two weeks of hard work. The attitude of those on the mainland appears to be: "Well, that's what you get for living in such a place"; but given that this is a British Isle and presumably has equal status with all other British Isles, it is not really good enough. Still, it's an improvement on what went before, and we can only hope that further improvements may eventually be achieved.

The caravans all came in on the first run the *Spes Clara* did to Papa Stour. This was a tremendously exciting day for us; as well as the caravans we had bought a twenty-year-old Land Rover. In the past we had relied on other people's tractors and trailers when we needed transport, but with the coming of the caravans it was definitely time to get a vehicle of our own. It has proved invaluable to us and to others on the island; it has carried coal, cow manure, seaweed, sand and shingle as well as people, and we use it to bring our holiday visitors and their baggage up from the pier. It is the only enclosed vehicle on the island and we are hired occasionally by the district nurse, the doctor and others to take them round the houses. It has also served more than once as an ambulance when we have had to take a patient to the airstrip in an emergency. Last year we sadly moved our oldest inhabitant to the airstrip when she broke her leg. Mother of eight, four of whom remain on the isle, at the age of 91 this was her first flight and her first visit to Lerwick for many, many years. Her leg took a long time mending and she faded and died in the hospital, but was brought back to the isle to be buried in the Papa Stour kirkyard. She was a stabilising influence in our small community and was respected by everyone. All my new babies were rocked in her arms as I took them to her house when they were just a few days old to be registered by her daughter, Mary, the Registrar for the island.

Once here the caravans were placed on concrete bases and made fast against the wind. It was fortunate that Kevin made a good job of it as five months later we had the worst wind we have ever had— Hurricane Flossie. There was a bad forecast in the morning, but we got plenty of bad forecasts; the wind rose steadily all through the day, and towards evening Kevin went down to the pier where his boat, the *Flying Fish*, was moored, to see how she was faring. There were four boats moored in Housa Voe, but only two were still in evidence when the hurricane abated the following day. The *Venture* survived as she has a deck shelter, and so did the *Skua*, a yacht with a cabin, but the two open boats, the *Sylvia* and the *Flying Fish* took in so much water that they sank. The *Sylvia*, a hundred-year-old, twenty-three foot Stroma yawl with a heavy diesel engine, sank to the bottom, while the *Flying Fish*, a nineteen-foot Shetland model, filled up and sank to her gunwales.

Once the gale took hold you couldn't see the boats for waves and spray, and it wasn't until the following day that we knew which boats had ridden out the storm and which had not. When the wind moderated Kevin was able to row off to the *Flying Fish* in the dinghy, tow her ashore and bale her out. Raising the *Sylvia* was far more of a problem; it was three days before the sea went down enough for them to tackle the job. With the aid of big inflatable buoys they attempted to raise her on her moorings—they got the bow up but could not raise the stern with the engine in it. Eventually the *Venture* towed the *Sylvia*, still on the bottom, across to the south side of Housa Voe to a sandy beach where they beached her on the high tide. A tractor with block and tackle drew her up, and as the tide ebbed she was visible for the first time for several days. The engine had to be completely stripped down in double quick time to clean the salt water out; apart from that she had sprung a few leaks, but considering the severity of the storm and the treatment she had had during her rescue, the damage she sustained was relatively slight.

Normally the walk from the pier to our house takes twenty minutes, but on the night of Hurricane Flossie it took Kevin an hour and a half to get home once he had decided there was nothing he could do about his boat. I was indoors with the children and although I knew it was blowing hard I had not realised that the strength of the wind was far more than we had ever experienced before. When I saw Kevin coming up the road I decided to go out and meet him and at the same time check up on the caravans to make sure they were still standing and that their fastenings were holding all right. They are held with wire round the chassis through concrete blocks set deep in the ground. As I ran round the end of the byre the wind got under my heels and I found myself scampering along helplessly in mid-air, unable to get my feet down on the ground. Eventually I was blown forward and slithered halfway across the yard on my tummy before coming to rest in stunned amazement at Kevin's feet. He was as surprised as I was to find me there. The caravans to our great relief were standing well, but with the wind blowing the way it was there was absolutely nothing we could do to make them any safer. After that we walked round and had a look at the roof of the byre, which we knew was in urgent need of renewal. As we stood gazing up at it a sheet of hundred-year-old corrugated iron came loose, and took off high across the garden.

The arrival of the caravans was greeted with mixed feelings by the other residents of Papa Stour. There were fears that the visitors would disturb the ubiquitous sheep and destroy the peacefulness of the island generally, but I do not think this has happened. Everyone else seems to enjoy meeting the new faces as much as we do.

As far as 'promoting' Papa Stour as an island paradise for tourists is concerned, I find I just cannot do it. The whole idea of 'catering for tourists' is a bit like selling one's birthright. I provide a roof over their heads, and the rest is up to them; if they cannot see the beauties of the place and enjoy it as it is then they must have chosen the wrong place. I do find myself apologising for the weather from time to time. It is good to come with a specific interest such as bird watching or nature study of any sort. Students sometimes come with their books and find it a good opportunity to get on with some work without the myriad distractions that assail them elsewhere.

We gain in a variety of ways from the caravans; it is lovely to see our children going out and finding new playmates amongst our visitors. We too have made a number of new friends and met many interesting people from a variety of specialised walks of life. But in spite of this, we are still in the position of looking forward to the hoped-for financial gains. Although many are attracted to the idea of an island holiday, few actually manage to get here; even from other parts of Shetland it is not easy, as we do not have a regular ferry service; one cannot just arrive at Sandness and expect to cross the Sound within half an hour. Visiting Shetland from farther afield is very expensive; one can fly from London to New York for far less than one can fly from London to Shetland. Added to this is the undoubted fact that most people in England look southwards when thinking in terms of a holiday; you need to be an original thinker to look north.

We continue to rack our brains for ways of making money. We can keep body and soul together but we certainly have no prospects of getting rich. We are currently involved in a mussel farming experiment; this consists of a small wooden raft which is moored in Hamna Voe, and we hope that tiny mussels will attach themselves to the ropes that hang from it and there grow big. After about eighteen months we should be able to harvest them and sell them, and if it is successful, larger rafts will be built, but this is never likely to be more than a sideline. In our rough waters spots sheltered enough to hold these rafts are few and far between.

Occasionally jobs of a temporary nature crop up: the road has to be repaired; some repair work needs doing at the school; someone who has come out of the hospital needs a home help. Jobs such as these are eagerly sought, and in the meantime we knit.

Crafts are thought of as an obvious source of income for people who live in isolated places where they are unable to find employment, but the lack of basic amenities frequently prevents us from following this form of employment here. One handicap is the fact that our regular communications with the outside world are infrequent, and another is the lack of mains electricity. One of our neighbours is a talented potter, but the four kilowatt generator she has, the largest on the isle, is not sufficient for her to have an electric kiln.

With the general lack of employment we must turn our thoughts to how to manage with a minimum of cash, and we must make the most of the resources we do have, thereby hopefully producing for ourselves some of the things which we do not have the money to buy.

Chapter 6
Self-sufficiency

In days gone by, when communities such as this were more self-sufficient, there were so many more pairs of hands available to do the work involved. There were sisters, aunts and grannies to do all the innumerable jobs which in my household would nowadays fall on me. One did the washing, another churned the butter, an older sister minded the infant, someone else milked the cow, and yet another did the cooking. No doubt being a mother has always been a very demanding and full-time job, but in those days women got far more support from their families who usually lived in the same district, and frequently in the same house.

I have chosen to reject many of the material artifacts that constitute twentieth century living, but where they do fit into my scheme of things, and can be used without harming the environment, I am not ashamed to use them. There is a school of thought which believes that isolated communities such as this should be retained as living museums. You can still see old-fashioned implements here and you can see people doing things in the old ways. But we cannot escape the twentieth century; we must select from it. Where the old ways are the best we continue to use them, and do not accept all new inventions as being improvements. Weed killers are a case in point, as they kill not only weeds but many quite harmless plants and small creatures, all of which have a part to play in keeping nature in balance. If we unbalance nature too far there is every likelihood that we will destroy our world.

Although we work on the assumption that we may one day have to be self-sufficient, at the same time we continue to press for better amenities. We get two deliveries of mail a week where others get two deliveries a day; in fact the mail boat goes three times a week, but apparently the post office can only afford to pay for two deliveries, so on Wednesdays we have to collect our letters from the post office on the island or let them lie there until Friday when they will be delivered along with Friday's mail.

Electricity is something we talk about a great deal. Whatever else we may not have we are never short of wind, and surely we should be using this for our electricity? A wind generator which provides for more than a couple of hundred watt lamps requires a capital outlay running into thousands of pounds, and two lamps is just not enough. I know I have had much more time to do productive and mindful things since I bought my washing machine, and when Kevin was making creels for the fishing he sawed more wood in two hours with a borrowed electric saw than he had previously sawn in two weeks by hand.

What I would like to see here is an experimental wind generator which could provide electricity for the whole community. It is sad that in the British Isles which have such a large coastal—and consequently windy—area the government has done so little research into wind power, but continues to pursue the nuclear policy, even though the world's stocks of uranium are known to be very limited and the hazards are known to be so great. Unfortunately British governments are not known for their ability to do an about-turn, but I would suggest to them that the wind will always be with us, and uranium will not.

Most of the houses on Papa Stour have their own diesel lighting plants; in some cases two houses share, and a few still use oil lamps. We have to bring in diesel in forty-five gallon drums, and do our own maintenance work on the generators—all of which is time-consuming. Ours is a three kilowatt plant, which means that it will take an automatic washing machine—just. I cannot do the very hot programmes as it is the heater which puts the strain on the generator, but it is definitely preferable to washing everything by hand for a family of five. Although we are up before daylight in the winter, no one ever has the light on in the morning. We manage with candles or a tilley lamp. It is the moving of the diesel fuel and the fact that a small engine cannot be run twenty-four hours a day that restricts us; it would be nice just to flick a switch like everyone else.

Most houses have a solid fuel stove for cooking; we cannot have electric cookers. Many also have a small calor gas cooker or a primus stove—useful for the quick cup of tea. Cooking on a solid fuel stove is an art in itself; you never know if you will be able to get the oven to the required temperature; the wind may suddenly die down and your fire cease to draw. To be efficient they require regular cleaning which is a dirty job; soot always accumulates and there is no clean way of removing it.

Most solid fuel stoves have a built-in back boiler, and this is how we get our hot water supply. Plumbing is something that not everyone would venture to tackle, and there are many houses here with no hot water system at all; they just have a large kettle or pot permanently on the stove. If someone were to take a bath whilst I was baking, this would be very unpopular as the oven temperature would drop like a stone, but apart from that it is a most excellent and economical way of getting a constant supply of hot water. And of course the stove heats the whole house and keeps it dry; our bedroom is over the kitchen, so it is never really cold up there. We have an open fire in the living room but we feel extravagant if we burn coal there, and tend to confine ourselves to the kitchen except on special occasions when we light a fire of driftwood.

Over much of Shetland there are vast quantities of peat which has been used as fuel for generations. It varies in quality, but the blue-black peat is as good as any coal and far cleaner to burn; it does not make soot. It is especially good for open fires and has a lovely smell. It works well in the solid fuel cooker too; but sadly Papa Stour does not have any peat: any turf that was here has been flayed off and burned long ago. Peat cutting rights have in the past been made available to the Papa folk on the mainland and on another island some distance away called Papa Little, and they used to import peat. They began to use coal in the second half of the last century, but the price has always been high in comparison with the incomes of the people here.

The art of cutting and curing peat demands a good deal of time, skill and hard labour. For several years we cut peat at Sandness. Choosing a fine, calm day, we would leave our boat lying off the Sandness pier, always a risky business as it is not a safe pier. Then we would walk the three miles up the hill to our peat bank and work through the day, stopping for a picnic lunch, then in the evening three miles down the hill again and back across the Sound. In the ensuing weeks after the peats have been cut they have to be raised—stood on end in little pyramids so that the wind can dry them, then they have to be turned so that the wind can dry the other side. After that we would put them into sacks and carry them down to the roadside, and finally we would hire a lorry to take them to the Sandness pier. By this time it was probably September and the weather was starting to deteriorate. The greatest number of bags our boat could carry was fifteen, so shipping them required several journeys; and we would often get them home a few bags at a time on the mail boat long after our boat was brought ashore for the winter. A year's supply of peat would be about three hundred bags, though we never cut anything like this number.

Obviously this was inefficient and unsatisfactory, but peat is there for the taking, and I would like to think that in years to come we shall become better organised for transport, and be able to supply at least some of our fuel needs from the peat bank.

In the meantime, coal is burned in all the houses, supplemented to a greater or lesser extent with driftwood. This depends on a person's enthusiasm for going around the banks beachcombing; and woe betide anyone who takes another's wood that has been put up to dry above the high tide line. This is theft. I am a fanatical beachcomber when I can find the time, and bring home all sorts of things in the hopes that I may one day find a use for them—the children always seem to welcome a new teapot for their garden parties. My best find was a tin of Brie in perfect condition. Driftwood comes in two categories: building wood and burning wood. Sometimes it takes years to find a use for a piece of building wood, but you would regret it if you burned it.

When we meet we describe our recent finds to each other, and old men yarn about the great finds of long ago. Barrels of spirits were not unknown, but in those cases the excise men would have been ready to pounce on anyone who failed to keep his mouth shut. Nowadays what was wood has often been replaced by plastic. During our few years here most of the fishing boats have gone over from wooden fishboxes to plastic ones. Plastic makes the beaches very unsightly and stays around for a long time. A fishbox is quite a good find as it has many uses; we have one for a toy box and another for a sandpit. In summer we sometimes go round the island by boat and fetch wood out of the geos which have high cliffs and are inaccessible from the land. We can bring home a good load in this way and really big logs can be towed behind the boat. I get great satisfaction from driftwooding, and as we sit by our blazing, spitting log fire on a winter's evening we reminisce about the adventures we had getting the wood. The salt makes the wood spit out sparks, and one has to beware of holes in socks and hearthrugs.

Trees only grow in Shetland where someone has made a great and prolonged effort to grow them, and then they are the oddest shapes, gnarled and bent by the everlasting gales. Timber has to be imported, and of course with freight charges the price of it is very high indeed, so driftwood does play a part in our building activities. There is considerable competition if wood is known to be coming in; we might hear that a coaster had lost its deck cargo in a storm. The direction of the wind is observed with keener interest than ever, and folk have been known to rise before dawn in order to be first at the banks.

Coal has more than trebled in price in the eight years we have lived on Papa Stour, and continues to rise. Only one grade is available in Shetland, and it varies considerably in quality. There is always a generous amount of dust in the bags.

Here I should mention one of the disadvantages of living on an island, and it applies not only to coal. If you order goods and receive poor quality material or even an alternative that you did not really want, it is hardly ever worthwhile to return it and get what you did want, because of the time and the expense involved. The thought of returning a ton of coal because there is too much dust in it is out of the question. We just have to take it and pay.

And now to the subject of food, demands for which never cease, as any mother with a growing family knows. We do grow a certain amount of our own food and are rarely without a selection of fresh vegetables. We were vaguely vegetarian when we came here, but soon found that if we were to survive we should eat whatever came our way. By this I mean particularly fish. Fish is one of the best sources of protein and should form part of every self-sufficient islander's diet. I do not have any qualms about killing and eating the flesh of other creatures; we must adapt ourselves to what food is available and sustain ourselves as best we can. I am not very happy about buying the meat of unknown animals from shops, although I do it now and then. I know many people would restrict their meat-eating habits if they had to kill the creature they wanted to eat and then remove its fur or feathers, take out its guts and chop off its head. I do all this with my hens, but I wouldn't want to do it every day, so meat is something we eat only occasionally. We fish from our own small boat in the summer, and if we are not fishing someone else frequently is and has a few to spare. The seine net boats use our pier from time to time and are always ready to give us a few of the smaller ones from their catch. Although crabs are not fished for, they are often caught in the lobster creels. Lobsters used to be abundant round here and still would be if it had been left to the islanders and their small boats, but bigger boats capable of working a hundred creels or more came, caught the lobsters and went away. Nowadays you have to be both daring and canny to catch lobsters. We rarely eat them; the price is so high that most people prefer to sell them. I like lobster very much but I cannot understand what makes people pay such very high prices for it in restaurants—unless it is to impress their business associates with their lavishness. I suspect lobster is mainly paid for from expense accounts.

I did not know what fresh fish was until I came to Papa Stour. The thought of school fish pie can still make me feel very ill, but a freshly caught mackerel rolled in oatmeal and fried is quite delicious, and the mackerel themselves are so beautiful, gleaming and glistening in iridescent shades of blue and green.

Crabs are tedious to prepare but well worth the time and trouble; we usually eat crab cold with mayonnaise made with the yolk of an egg. I cannot think of a nicer meal for a summer evening than crab sandwiches with home-made brown bread and home-made mayonnaise and a salad of crisp cos lettuce leaves from the garden.

The most common fish around our shores is the piltock, or young saithe. They could almost be described as Papa Stour's national dish. We eat them fresh, but they can also be salted and dried and kept through the winter in a dry place. Dried piltocks are very popular with the local folk who eat them boiled with potatoes and served with plenty of butter. Small piltocks called sillocks can be caught off the rocks with a rod, or wand as they say here. Winter evenings are the best time for this, just as it is getting dark, and you need an offshore breeze. Sometimes little bigger than sprats, they are very palatable, especially as fresh fish is scarce in the winter.

We have been successful with a variety of vegetables—though as far as greens are concerned only the Shetland cabbage will withstand the rigours of the salty storms of winter. Root crops do well: we always have plenty of potatoes, carrots, swedes and beetroot. Peas and broad beans can do well if we get a warm summer. At the end of one cold and wet summer I was standing sadly surveying my fine rows of peas which had hundreds of pods on. The pods had not filled: it was September, storms were brewing and I knew the peas would never swell now. All that work for nothing. I felt very disappointed. But suddenly an idea struck me—surely I'd seen it in a book somewhere—pea pod wine! So I hastily picked a bucket of pods before the gale started and went inside to consult my books. The result wasn't perfect, but it had the desired effect, for it was alcoholic. I am blessed with a husband who will try absolutely anything in this line, and my problem is to keep the wine from him long enough for it to achieve at least some degree of maturity. He is however very appreciative and encouraging, and I have become fired with enthusiasm for home winemaking as a result of this first experiment with the pea pods. I have since made a brew of nettle beer, which was easy and needed to be drunk after two weeks, so it presented no marital strife. I hope to make a lot more of that in the future. The nettles must be picked in the early part of the summer before they get that jaded look about them.

Where we cannot grow the food we need we buy it in bulk. Flour and cereals come in sacks, and we make all our own wholemeal bread. Much to my daughter's delight a visitor recently brought us a loaf of white shop bread as a treat for her. We shall see whether the children will want to maintain their wholefood eating habits when they grow up. At present anything from the shop, such as cornflakes or baked beans, is regarded as a treat. I strongly believe in eating what I think of as real food, food which has not been heavily processed and loaded with additives and preservatives, but it is difficult to prove, especially to a child, that their bodies will be stronger and healthier and their heads clearer if they eat whole foods. I am convinced however that too many sweets produces a bad-tempered brat with rotten teeth, and consequently these are strictly rationed.

We acquired our first hens when we were living in the caravan. I bought half a dozen from a battery farmer on the mainland; although only about eighteen months old, they were worn out as far as he was concerned. Hens start laying (with no help from a cock I discovered) when they are six or seven months old; they lay for about a year, then moult; in succeeding years they will lay fewer and fewer eggs each year. The ones we bought arrived in absolutely miserable condition and confirmed everything I suspected about battery farming. One had so few feathers that she was promptly christened Oven Ready. For the first few days they did not venture out of their house; they had never seen the light of day and green grass was certainly a new experience for them. They didn't know how to scratch. They got their new feathers in due course and learned to behave more or less like normal free ranging hens. Oven Ready became very beautiful with magnificent glossy feathers in shades of gold and chestnut, but she never recovered from the laryngitis she brought with her and died a few months later. The others eventually started laying, and I started learning that to get eggs out of a hen you must put plenty of food into it.

I now think that it is better to keep hens in a fairly confined space. It may be that they do not expend so much energy going for long walks; they certainly lay more eggs. We have built a mobile ark with a run attached to a design supplied by the Henry Doubleday Research Association, and we move this about daily on rough parts of the garden. The hens have ample opportunity to scratch, and they are working for us clearing the ground and manuring it at the same time. As long as they are moved regularly I think they are quite happy like this.

One of the hazards of free ranging was that in the summer the hens used to lay their eggs in patches of nettles in the distant corners of our domain. Looking for them took a long time and involved dressing up in trousers and boots, but coming upon a stash of a dozen eggs that you didn't know you had can be very satisfying.

After a year with the five remaining battery hens I bought some pullets at six weeks old, and when they started to lay they were far more productive than the battery hens. I now keep about ten hens and a cock. Each year one or two go broody and we get some babies. We eat the young cockerels when they are about six months old; they are delicious, plump and succulent at this age, and it usually coincides with our Christmas feastings. Old hens also get eaten when they no longer seem to be pulling their weight; these require long slow cooking in a casserole, but their years of scratching around have given them an excellent flavour.

I buy in food for the hens though I am hopeful that one day I shall no longer need to. They get household and vegetable scraps as well of course, and fish heads and crab shells; but too much fish makes fishy-tasting eggs. Mackerel does not have as fishy a taste as piltocks, and I have salted down a barrel of mackerel and successfully fed them on this, well soaked, then boiled and mixed with potatoes. If they are to lay eggs they need plenty of protein.

Poultry manure is too strong to use on its own on the garden, but when I clean out the chicken house I put the manure into the compost heap and the result is very satisfactory.

The heaviest time for laying is March, April, May and June. During these months, when we have a surplus of eggs I preserve some in waterglass. I put down a few every day until I have filled my container; this holds about a hundred eggs in the liquid (waterglass can be obtained from chemists), and we eat these during October, November and December when the hens are moulting and fresh eggs are scarce. Preserved eggs are not as nice as fresh ones, but they do perfectly well for baking and we make omelets and quiches with them.

Clothing the family does not seem to pose any great problem; we are lucky in that friends on the mainland seem to regard us as an ideal dumping ground for their cast-off clothing. I don't mind this at all as I prefer old clothes to new ones. As the children get older I suppose there will come a time when they are not content with other people's cast-offs. This is an area in which Grannies are very helpful, and our children just have to be content with getting a parcel from a Granny now and then. I have noticed that when they do get new clothes they go around announcing to everyone that their trousers or whatever it happens to be are 'brand new' as opposed to 'new', which really means that they are someone else's old ones. We do knit brand new jumpers for them on the knitting machine, and often these are stripey ones as we use up the oddments of wool left over from orders. The only real expense is footwear, and especially wellingtons which we all wear nearly all the time when we are out of doors. Sometimes I think it would be better if the children wore their shoes outside, but that is invariably the day they choose to play in the burn. In bygone days of course bare feet were common amongst the children and that was a matter of necessity more than choice. They also wore rivlins, slippers made out of home-cured sealskin or cow hide, but poor living conditions and inadequate clothing have resulted in tuberculosis taking its toll in the past. I would like to see my children go barefoot more often, but one step on a thistle will put them off the idea for the rest of the summer.

Although we often hear about people practising self-sufficiency, it is treated by the media mainly as a rather peculiar cult. This is because the advertising part of the media, which undoubtedly carries a lot of weight, is always telling us that there is no need for us to be self-sufficient: if we work, work, work, we will have enough money to spend, spend, spend; but for me happiness does not lie that way. Whether it be a jumper or a turnip, everything we make or grow ourselves—whilst it may not be the perfect shape—gives us a certain amount of satisfaction. Eating an egg from one of my own hens is preferable to a shop egg, and I have the added satisfaction of having, indirectly, produced it myself.

The other side of self-sufficiency is that we do without a number of things that others regard as necessary. This applies especially to food; we eat what we have. Not for us a trip to the supermarket to buy frozen strawberries in January. We have periods of glut and periods of shortage. We have been known to eat mackerel and mushrooms (together) three times a day and at the same time I was frantically drying and bottling mushrooms and pickling mackerel. As far as cooking goes, if pressed I feel I can almost make something out of nothing now. Our first winter here was a difficult one as we didn't have very much food; we shared a sack of flour, a sack of brown rice and a sack of soya beans with our friends, and we filched an occasional cabbage leaf. We are unlikely ever to eat another soya bean; they are *dull*. It was then that I learned to make Zenburgers—rissoles made out of anything available (cooked soya beans in our case), an onion if you have one, the magic ingredient being a liberal sprinkling of curry powder. Another 'nothing' meal is comfrey fritters; I have quite a big comfrey bed here, it grows well and I use it for green manure. Fresh young comfrey leaves are not particularly palatable raw, being hairy and of a peculiar flavour, but in a batter made with brown flour, egg and milk and fried in deep hot oil they are crisp and delicious, and no doubt the comfrey does us all good.

Self-sufficiency means managing with what you have; on Papa Stour I sometimes think we carry this rather too far. If time were money, then the time we spend repairing worn-out equipment would make those articles very costly. I suppose we have the time but not the money, or at least we have more time than people on the mainland. A new tractor costs well into five figures now, but the tractors on Papa Stour would have been bought at the lower end of the three figure bracket, and they have all had numerous decokes, rebores, resleeves, new pistons, rings; in fact practically everything in them has probably been replaced at some time or other. A new tyre is one you get off someone else's old tractor when it has made its final pronouncement that it can go no farther. Fences too are patched and patched. New fencing is very expensive, and although financial assistance is available in the form of grants, many people are put off by the amount of paperwork involved and the general difficulty we find in dealng with officials who seem to live in a different world from us. In fact you have to buy the fencing materials yourself, do the work, have it inspected and then get the grant payment; if you are short of capital this can make application for a grant virtually impossible with the high interest rates on loans today. We are not agri-business farmers; they appear to operate on huge overdrafts acquired on the assumption of large proceeds from sales of crops or livestock in the back end of the year. Here we prefer to do without if we cannot pay for it. So a roll of fencing wire is bought to cover a gap, a few stabs are split from a log found on the beach—the price of a new fence post bought in Shetland would astonish any English farmer.

Personally, the ways of business do not appeal to me; financial assistance from the government and banks to get a business off the ground are all very well, but there is a tremendous amount of stress involved in borrowing large sums of money; indeed you cannot call your soul your own and are forever answerable to the lender until the debt is paid. Life just gets too difficult and the joy of it is not there any more. Perhaps I lack ambition; I know we have to strive, but I shall not be striving in the world of loans and overdrafts. I want to enjoy my life.

Chapter 7

Papa Stour – the microcosm

Our very isolation makes us a community—one of the great things about living on an island is that it is a miniature world. Thanks to the native Shetlanders who have remained, Papa Stour has a fairly stable community, and it is their permanence that I admire and envy. Many people think nothing these days of moving to a different part of the country every few years—a change of jobs or just a desire to be near friends or relatives causes them to uproot themselves and start again with fresh relationships in a new community. But you can't get very far in just a few years. Many of the people here had ancestors as far back as they can go living on this island. Two girls live down the road, the younger one being much the same age as my boys; they live with their father and grandfather, both born on the isle. I feel they have something very solid behind them in a place they can call their own. After eight years here I am beginning to feel something of the strength this permanence can bring, but almost half of my life has already been spent elsewhere. Having been moved around so much as a child myself I am not anxious to subject my own children to it.

Each person here is known as an individual and makes a contribution to the community as a whole. It may be a continuous and positive contribution such as that made by the boatmen; on occasions it is a negative one, but it all combines to form the life of the island. We thrash out our own problems without recourse to the courts. When a window at the school was accidentally broken by some reveller, after a party, that person saw to the repair of it the following day. He could hardly do otherwise. Each person counts, and their comings and goings are the stuff of my life; almost daily in fair weather or foul I see a figure striding along the skyline to the east of my house—that's Jessie counting her sheep;

another smaller figure trudges up from the beach with a bundle of driftwood—it's my neighbour, Helen. She's as old as the century and still goes about her croft and minds a few sheep. Yet if I passed these people in Lerwick they would just merge into the crowd; here they are real individuals, and I hope I am one too.

Cooperation happens when it is needed, but on the whole people work individually, giving help when they are asked or when they can see that it is urgently needed. When the coal is brought in by the *Spes Clara* everyone with a tractor and trailer turns out to deliver it to the houses that have no transport. If a boat owner needs to lay a mooring it calls for strong hands, and as everyone on the island knows the necessity for sea transport they will always help to ensure the safety of a boat. In the same way, when the small boats are brought ashore at the end of the summer, several men will go down to help in the work of pulling the boats up the beach to their winter noosts.

If there is an accident or someone is suddenly taken seriously ill, almost everyone on the island is temporarily brought together in close cooperation. It was eight o'clock on a November night with a force nine north-easterly gale blowing when the doctor on the mainland decided, after a number of telephone conversations, that he would have to come in and see a woman who was in considerable distress. The only way he could possibly get here was with the Aith lifeboat. At nine o'clock the lifeboat appeared at the Papa pier and the doctor leapt ashore. As luck would have it the north-easterly is the one wind to which our pier is open, so the lifeboat lay off until the doctor's return. Nobody at this time had a vehicle with headlights, so he travelled the mile-and-a-half from the pier to the patient's house on the back of a tractor, whilst the driver drove with one hand and held a feeble torch with the other.

There was no telephone at the patient's house, and as their next door neighbour my phone was constantly ringing with information and messages. Concern emanated from everybody I spoke to, and I could feel that everyone on the island had their minds on that particular local crisis that night. The husband of the sick woman had been dashing in and out throughout the day to telephone the doctor and was rapidly becoming overcome, not just by his wife's illness but by the drama of the whole affair. They were new to the isle and did not know many people; on a pitch black winter's night with the wind blowing fiercely and the knowledge that medical help really wasn't within easy reach, minds can become a little unbalanced.

Having seen the patient, the doctor decided she needed hospital treatment, and most fortuitously a number of people were in the adjacent schoolroom having a rehearsal for a Christmas entertainment; someone dashed down to the coastguard hut at the other end of the isle for a stretcher, and the rehearsing musicians were enlisted as stretcher bearers. I supplied a fur coat and hat, the patient was wrapped up and lashed onto the stretcher, and they set off for the pier. Walking in a severe gale demands a certain amount of concentration, but in the normal course of events one would never try to carry something large in a wind. A tractor and trailer would have been the only alternative but the doctor rejected this, as the bumps sustained by the patient lying in an unsprung trailer would have aggravated her condition. As they reached the pier the lifeboat came alongside again with floodlight blazing; in a matter of seconds doctor and patient were safely on board and stowed away below and the boat was away.

It has not always been like this; we must be very thankful for telephones and for the National Health Service which pays for these emergencies. The telephone here is a radio link, but before this was installed a neighbour of ours recalls how as a child he broke his ankle and his father spent hours signalling across the Sound to Sandness through the night with a tilley lamp to summon help. Even so, this help did not come until well into the following day when a fishing boat called in to see what it was all about. The boy was taken away to hospital where he had to stay alone and away from his family for many weeks.

The fact that there are no medical facilities at all on the island does present problems and dangers. Emergency services are good, and in the event the doctor on the mainland can call on Loganair or the lifeboat for transport to the island. What we do not have is a regular surgery where a person who is feeling off colour can call in and have a check-up; an elderly person who has had an operation cannot receive a regular visit from a District Nurse just to make sure that a full recovery is in progress. Sometimes the doctor comes down to meet the boat at the Sandness pier. Whilst pregnant I once had a check-up on the banks at Sandness. I lay on the grass above the beach whilst the doctor inspected my lump. It didn't bother me a bit, but I think he was a little embarrassed, concerned perhaps that someone might come along and disapprove. For the last few years I have been in charge of a small supply of medicines provided by the doctor. Most of us when ill consult the doctor by telephone and he will prescribe if necessary on the basis of a telephone diagnosis. Infections are automatically treated with antibiotics, and I also have a supply of cough mixture and tummy upset mixture. More recently, and only after several requests from people with toothache and other severe pains, I have received a supply of painkillers. This does help, as in the winter it could take a week or two for medicine to reach here if the doctor had to send them in specifically when an illness arose. A surgery on the island once a month might be a good idea.

Three years ago Kevin became ill over a period of time. We don't know when it started; he just seemed to slow down, he slept more and worked less. I had three infants under four years old at the time, I was breast-feeding the youngest, and regrettably I really did not apply myself to observing his trouble. Eventually he got up one morning and announced he was going to the mainland to see the doctor. He wasn't really able to describe what he felt—he just didn't feel right.

It was summer, so arranging for a boat to take him to Sandness and return later to bring him home wasn't too much of a problem. The doctor gave him a check-up and announced that his blood-pressure was very high indeed. He returned home with the news that he would be going to hospital in Aberdeen in a few days' time for tests. It was assumed, quite wrongly as it turned out, that there was something wrong with his kidneys; kidney failure was mentioned, and there was talk of an operation to remove a kidney which might be diseased. Fortunately all these fears turned out to be unfounded, but not before I had hastily weaned my youngest and made arrangements for a friend from the mainland to come and look after the three children whilst I went to Aberdeen to be with Kevin when he had his operation. Communications with the medical profession are not my strong point. As well as wondering if he might die I started thinking about what we would have to do if he was no longer going to be a fit man. We couldn't continue living on Papa Stour—that was for sure. There is a shortage of able-bodied men as it is, and the young must help the old and the single women—getting in the fuel supplies, helping with heavy work on the crofts and so on. We could hardly expect to live here and receive that sort of help ourselves for the rest of our lives. We would have to leave the island. The thought made my heart sink. Where on earth would we go? What would we do? All I knew was that I didn't want to be anywhere else.

Fortunately my fears turned out to be unnecessary; we are still here, Kevin is able to work, and we have consolidated our feelings that this is the right place for us. It has also taught me lessons about taking people for granted and about the value of good health. Health is of the utmost importance and we should do everything we can to ensure that we maintain it. Friends were marvellous at this time, and I received help and support from many, many people. The children were really not old enough to know what was happening, but when we walked down the road to the pier on that sunny morning to meet the boat bringing Kevin back after five long weeks in hospital the children must have known that our family was complete once again.

Months later I discovered that he has something which is called essential hypertension—this means inexplicably high blood pressure, and not very much is known about what causes it or how it can best be treated. We did meet one doctor who told us that lobster fishermen were prone to it on account of their very exciting and dangerous way of life.

We were told that he would have to take tablets for the rest of his life, but the dosage is considerably reduced now, and as a more natural method of dealing with the high blood pressure we have taken up meditation. We both learned T.M. a few months after he was in hospital; it is, as far as we are concerned, a relaxation technique, and the benefits are firstly physical and subsequently mental. We are sure it has helped to maintain his blood pressure at a reasonable level, and it has helped us both to order our lives better.

There is an excellent air ambulance service operating in Shetland, but as far as Papa Stour is concerned this is restricted by the inadequacies of our airstrip and the vagaries of the weather. The airstrip resembles a very rough piece of moorland in which all the boulders have been pushed to one side; it is level and fairly well drained but it does need a proper surface. The only plane which can land here is the Islander, which must be the Land Rover of the air.

So planes do not land here very often; it's a rare enough event for the children to be allowed out of school to see it. When we hear that one is coming we dash up to the airstrip and hang up the windsock which we keep in our byre; its expanse of luminous orange marks the spot in an otherwise bleakly uniform part of the island. I always get a lump in my throat watching the plane take off with someone who matters to me on board, for in our small community every single person matters.

One summer the teacher arranged an outing for the school-children to the neighbouring island of Foula. We can see this isolated isle which has the highest cliffs in Britain to the south-west of here, but the boat journey is long and there is almost always a bad swell as you go farther out into the Atlantic. So a plane was chartered for the school trip and arrived at our airstrip on a bright and sunny morning. The children could hardly contain themselves; the six of them were strapped in, the naughtiest beside the teacher, and the tiny plane taxied to the end of the runway and started her take-off. Within ten minutes we had a telephone call from Foula to say they had arrived safely. The children spent two days on Foula climbing their high hills (Papa Stour is flat by comparison) and getting to know the Foula children, and coming back by plane three days later they were even luckier with their flight: not only did the pilot make an aerial tour of the island, but he flew out three miles to the west of Papa Stour to the notorious Ve Skerries where a new lighthouse was being built. This lighthouse marks a very dangerous line of rocks where in the past ships have been wrecked and lives lost. Only two years ago an Aberdeen trawler, the *Eleanor Viking*, went on the Ve Skerries on a stormy November night in bad visibility. This was the first time anyone has ever been known to be saved from a wreck on the Ve Skerries; miraculously all eight men were winched aboard a rescue helicopter whilst their boat was breaking up around them. In 1930 another Aberdeen boat, the *Ben Doran*, ran onto these rocks, but fishing boats did not have wireless in those days and although the wreck was discovered and several boats went out to try and give assistance, not one of them could get close to the wreck because of the heavy seas. A man from the Shetland boat *Smiling Morn* was determined to try to swim to the *Ben Doran* with a rope, but his companions forcibly prevented him, knowing full well that no human being could survive in those raging mountainous waves. Sick at heart the watchers turned at last away from the scene, as they could no longer bear to watch the doomed men clinging to the masts of their fast-disappearing boat. In the case of the *Eleanor Viking*, the Aith lifeboat stood by, but as with the *Ben Doran* she could not get close enough to render any assistance, so it was left to the helicopter and her brave crew to make the rescue from up above. This helicopter crew has since received many awards for bravery as a result of the *Eleanor Viking* rescue.

One of the focal points in the community is the school, which was closed when we first came to Papa Stour, but others have come, our own children are now starting, and happily the school has become a going concern. We have a full-time teacher occupying the schoolhouse, and she and her husband have settled comfortably into the life of the community. In the past there seems to have been an attitude that the teacher was slightly superior to other folk—whether this was felt by the teacher or by the islanders or both I'm not sure, but one gets the impression that the relationship in many isolated communities wasn't entirely a comfortable one; the fact that the job was often combined with that of missionary may have had something to do with it. Our teacher and her husband are both Geordies from north-east England, which adds another dimension to our mixed community; with all the children but one of English parents it cannot be said to be a typical Shetland school. But it is a typical jolly little primary school, and the schoolroom is always buzzing with exciting projects—making things, music and pictures—and they learn to read and do sums quite painlessly as well. The children all love the school, and although they respect their teacher, Mrs. Buggy, I believe they also think of her as a friend; some of them have been heard to address her as 'mum' whilst in deep concentration over some difficult task. School dinners are cooked on the premises by her husband, Joe, and he also provides dinners for some of the old age pensioners. These are known as 'meals on heels' as he dashes across the fields with his box of hot dinners before serving the children with theirs. The schoolroom is very old-fashioned with a high ceiling, an old pot-bellied stove and high windows designed so that the children could not see out and be distracted. By degrees, though not without constant pressure, new equipment and furniture is being obtained for the school, and the teacher has redecorated the room herself after waiting over a year for the authorities to do it. With the large influx in population in Shetland brought about by oil developments, the local authority is stretched to its utmost; pressure is far greater in the heavily populated areas, and sad to say nobody seems to have much in the way of energy or resources left to spend on Papa Stour and its tiny community.

We have no community hall, so the schoolroom is used for meetings and parties. We have had wedding feasts with full-scale meals where the women have got together beforehand and planned lavish and outlandish menus, each person providing whatever they had available. I might cook one of my chickens, another would prepare a large number of crabs, someone else would produce some smoked mackerel; meals of amazing proportions have been built up in this way with a main course fully adorned with vegetables, salads and sauces, followed by a variety of desserts and finally cups of tea and coffee. Nights of music and jollity have followed these feasts, with amateur bands ranging from Shetland fiddlers through guitars and drums to stirring choruses of inebriated singers. We have had slide shows, pantomimes have been performed, we have seen displays of modern creative dance, we've even played bingo. It's spontaneous and fun; we seem to make a point of enjoying ourselves.

Although the Church of Scotland kirk on Papa Stour is still used, it is some time since it played any real part in the life of the community, probably since Denis and Stella Shepherd left in 1970. He was the missionary or lay preacher and Mrs. Shepherd was the teacher; the job finished when the youngest island child became old enough to go to the high school in Lerwick, so the school was closed, they left the island and subsequently took up similar jobs across the Sound in Sandness.

When we first came to the isle a mainland minister or missionary would come in regularly throughout the summer to hold a Sunday service. Although I feel I am in sympathy with Christian ideas, on a bright summer Sunday morning I found myself closer to a religious experience on a walk to a high hill or gazing out from a high cliff top over a sparkling blue sea with fulmars gliding silently about, than sitting in the little kirk listening to a sermon.

One of the great dangers in a small community is gossip. We didn't know anything about this when we first came and unwittingly became involved in all sorts of intrigues of whose existence we were totally unaware. Someone tells you something, you make a comment and later on your comment is repeated in a slightly different way or with a different emphasis, and whilst it may well have been a very idle comment someone may decide to make something of it and feelings can become heated. One's business does tend to be everybody's business. For instance, if I were to tell someone that I was going to the mainland for a few days, practically everyone on the island would know within twenty-four hours, and then the speculation would start. Is she going to the dentist? Shopping? Just a holiday? And if there is a chance of a sinister reason somebody somewhere might think that one up too.

When we arrived on the isle the community was in a state of up-roar, and I'm sure we added to it. No doubt the islanders did feel threatened by such a sudden influx of people; newcomers seemed to be arriving by almost every boat, and the Land Court to settle the dispossession of some of the absentee crofters was imminent. It was at the time that boatloads of Pakistani immigrants were arriving on the south coast of England, and someone here must have made the chance remark that it seemed as if the Pakistanis were coming, for when this notion reached me I was told that Kevin and I were thought to be Pakistanis. This is just one example of how a remark can get completely out of hand, and it also showed me that people were talking about me, something I hadn't ex-perienced before. Remarks that could be described as negative are the worst, as negativity seems to snowball and very soon we are all sunk in gloom and depression. When this happens we all have to withdraw, reconsider and change the subject.

We all like to know what is going on, but the giving out of opinions should be avoided wherever possible, and one should never criticise for this will sound far worse when repeated by some-one else. I hope I have learned to guard my tongue and to keep my imaginative speculations to myself. Of course this goes on in all communities, large and small, but our isolation means that any situation may be gone into in the minutest detail and small issues seem like big ones, where in a larger community the many distrac-tions would prevent this.

If Kevin had written this contribution to *Living on an Island* you would have gained a very different picture, for the simple reason that he is a man and I am a woman. It is surprising in the 1980s to find the roles of the sexes as clearly defined as they are on Papa Stour. Men go out on boats, women stay at home, keep hot meals ready in the oven and look after the bairns. It is largely a matter of physical strength; there's not much point in my going to Sandness to collect half a dozen sacks of flour that I can't even lift. Whilst a man can cook and look after children, on Papa Stour it is often impossible for women to do men's work; of course there are women who are as strong as men, but for a man to live here he has to be physically strong—he's not going to get someone else to carry his loads.

Part of the trouble is that the population is so small and the houses are scattered; we are always short-handed. There are no teenagers or young single people here. There is a girl of eleven at the school and a boy of ten, and very shortly they will have to go to the high school on the mainland. That is the beginning of their leaving Papa Stour. Whilst they will come home for their holidays and for weekends in the summer term, the bulk of their lives will from then on be spent elsewhere, and it is unlikely that once grown up they will settle on Papa Stour. They have had a beautiful start in life, but a good education and life in the town is hardly likely to make them want to return to subsistence farming or a hand-to-mouth existence such as ours.

I have talked to Shetland folk who left Papa Stour in the 1950s and 60s. Some missed their children so badly when they left to go to the mainland school that they decided to leave the island too. Others went to help their youngsters find jobs and start to make their own way in life. Economic pressures were probably strong too; even before the oil there would have been a better chance of employment on the mainland than there could ever be on Papa Stour.

This problem is undoubtedly going to beset us in the years to come, and we do not know how we or our children will cope with it. They have to go at the age of twelve. Will we too leave the island then? I doubt it. Having found what I regard as my place in this world I want to hold onto it; I have made a commitment here and I want to stick to it. But none of us can say what lies ahead. The problem of the children leaving is five years away and I am enjoying the present—I have little hands to hold in the meantime.

Papa Stour is the centre of my particular world, and I have settled here and put down my roots. I feel a great love for the place and would like to see its people live in harmony and prosperity. The fact that the population has become so low means that there is hardly enough manpower here to generate anything new; I believe that to be viable the island needs more people, but knowing the difficulties and the state of mind that these induce one cannot be optimistic. It's not hopelessness but the recognition that you can never achieve as much as you would like to.

Better communications would certainly help; agriculture could be pursued in a more enterprising way if the problems of selling and shipping stock were overcome. Shetland hovers between the sublime and the ridiculous: whilst the port of Sullom Voe has tug boats, pilot boats, pollution boats all equipped with every imaginable electronic device, the island community of Papa Stour comes and goes with a privately owned, twenty-five foot open boat whose only navigational aid is a compass.

The beauty of my surroundings never fails to lift up my spirit. It's all out there—just in front of my windows: the Sound of Papa with the two holms of Forewick and Melby standing like sentinels for the boats to pass between, and the cliffs and hills of the mainland on the other side. Its moods are many, but I know that it can never fail to present me with a view of breathtaking beauty, which is confirmation of the fact that there is nothing more inspiring than the world of Nature. I'll stay with the Sound of Papa and the song of the skylark.

Biography

Ruth Wheeler was born in Durham, attended school there and went on to study History and Music before teaching in Birmingham and Brighton. In 1974 she came, with her family, to a croft on Egilsay, where they learned to cope with the rigours of life in a small, isolated community. She has three children, two of whom are adopted. Many of her articles have appeared in newspapers and magazines and she was a contributor to the recent US publication, *Shelter 2.* She is currently working on a collection of short stories about island life.

Vicki Coleman was born in 1939; much of her childhood was spent in rural East Anglia and although London attracted her as a young secretary eager to see the world, city life is definitely not for her. After travelling in Europe, the Middle East and Africa (where she met her husband Kevin), she found they could not easily settle down in England and headed for the Highlands of Scotland in search of a more challenging way of life. This they found on the tiny Shetland island of Papa Stour where along with other incomers thay have set about increasing the dwindling population; their three children and a number of others have caused the local authority to reopen the island school, and an island that was once in grave danger of depopulation now has a stable and growing community.